Hair Braiding to Grow, Strengthen, and Lengthen Your Hair

Written and Illustrated
by Diana K. Mitchell

Jones Bush & Ward Publishing Co., Inc.

Concord, North Carolina

Hair Braiding to Grow, Strengthen, and Lengthen Your Hair
Copyright © 2019 by Diana Kay Mitchell

All rights reserved. No part of this book, or ebook, may be used or reproduced by any means, graphic, electronic, or mechanical, including photocopying, recording, taping or by any information storage retrieval system without the written permission of the publisher.

Jones Bush & Ward Publishing Co., Inc.
P.O. Box 7566
Concord, NC 28027
www.jbwardpublishing.com

The Scripture quotations contained herein are from the New Revised Standard Version Bible, copyright © 1989, by the Division of Christian Education of the National Council of the Churches of Christ in the U.S.A., and are used by permission. All rights reserved.

Because of the dynamic nature of the Internet, any Web addresses or links contained in this book may have changed since publication and may no longer be valid.

The views expressed in this work are solely those of the author and do not necessarily reflect the views of the publisher, and the publisher hereby disclaims any responsibility for them.

This book was previously published as *The Hair Braider's Secret Reference Manual* under ISBNs 978-0-595-52350-4, and 978-0-9826503-0-1. Editorial changes and additions made to the work for the 2019 publication prompted a change in title to *Hair Braiding to Grow, Strengthen, and Lengthen Your Hair*.

For the 2022 publication of the ebook version of this work, some titles were expanded in order to accommodate screen readers. In addition, the table of contents, "Illustration Groups," was incorporated into the main Table of Contents. To maintain consistency between the paperback and the ebook versions, the ISBN for the paperback version was changed from 978-0-9826503-1-8 to the ISBN below.

Library of Congress Control Number: 2019954125

ISBN: 978-0-9826503-8-7 (pbk)
ISBN: 978-0-9826503-7-0 (ebook)

Printed in the United States of America

Text and illustrations copyright © 2019 by Diana Kay Mitchell

In loving memory of my mother, Geneva.

*I can still hear you saying to me,
"Diana, God can do anything, anything but fail!"*

I love and miss you, still.

*Love,
Daughter Diana*

Hair Braiding to Grow, Strengthen, and Lengthen Your Hair

This page has been intentionally left blank.

Table of Contents

Title Page i

Copyright ii

Dedication iii

Acknowledgments ix

Message to My Readers xi

How to Read this Book xiii
    Disclaimer Information xiii
    Understanding Textual Notations xiv
    How to Read Instructional Information xiv
    Editorial Changes xv
    Quick Thought Check #1 xviii

Chapter 1 | Understanding My African Hair 19
    Becoming "Hair Conscious" 20
    Your Hair Is Your Crown 23
    Brief Reflection on African American Hair and Braiding 24
    Materials You Will Need 28
    Some Things to Think About 29
    Quick Thought Check #2 30

Chapter 2 | Step One: The Preparation 31
    Preparing the Fiber 32
    Preparing Your Hair 33
    Δ Preventing Hairline Breakage 36
    Some Things to Think About 37
    Quick Thought Check #3 38

Chapter 3 | Step Two: Methods of Braiding and Extending Your Hair 39
    Quick Thought Check #4 41
    African Braiding Illustrated 42
    African Braiding Instructions 43
    Preparing the Cut Bulk 44
    Δ Fiber Has Weight 44
    Extending African Braids 45

African Braiding Versus French Braiding 51
French Braiding Illustrated 52
French Braiding Instructions 53
Extending French Braids 53
Plaiting Your Hair 57
Underhand Plaiting Illustrated 58
Underhand Plaiting Instructions 59
Overhand Plaiting Illustrated 60
Overhand Plaiting Instructions 61
Extending Plaits 61
Some Things to Think About 68

Chapter 4 | Step Three: Braid Care   69
Hair Ornaments and Styling 70
Daily Care 71
Weekly Care 72
Δ   Rebraiding 73
Δ   Brushing Your Hair Again 78
The Afro 78
Working with Hairstylists 80
Some Things to Think About 81
Quick Thought Check #5 82

Chapter 5 | A Brief Recap   83
Things to Remember 83
Hair Braiding Tips 85
The Secret to Growing Longer Hair 86
Some Things to Think About 88

Chapter 6 | A Bald-Headed Woman   89
Cosmetology as a Career Choice 91
Final Thoughts 92

Chapter 7 | Gallery of Hairstyles: Designs for Work, School, and Play   93
Slice, Strip, and Strands Illustrated 94
Slice, Strip, and Strands Explained 95
Anatomy of a Hairstyle Illustrated: Hairstyle 1 96

Table of Contents

   Anatomy of a Hairstyle Explained 97
      Hairstyle 2 98
      Hairstyle 3 99
      Hairstyle 4 100
      Hairstyle 5 101
      Hairstyle 6 102
      Hairstyle 7 103
      Hairstyle 8 104
      Hairstyle 9 105
      Hairstyle 10 106
   Quick Thought Check #6 108
   Your Personal Hair-Care Diary 109
      Calendar Example 110
      Milestone Notes Example 111
      Year One Calendar 112
      Year One Milestone Notes 113
      Year Two Calendar 114
      Year Two Milestone Notes 115
      Year Three Calendar 116
      Year Three Milestone Notes 117
      Your Hairstyles and Notes 118

Glossary   *125*
   Quick Thought Check #7 130

Further Reading and Study   *131*

Index   *135*

Hair Braiding to Grow, Strengthen, and Lengthen Your Hair

This page has been intentionally left blank.

Acknowledgments

I was blessed to have the first printed edition of my book, *The Hair Braider's Secret Reference Manual*, reviewed by the following people: Mr. Curtis Davis, COO, BioCare Labs; Dr. Eunice M. Dudley, Dudley Products, Inc., and Dudley Beauty School System; and, Mr. John Paul DeJoria, Chairman and CEO, John Paul Mitchell Systems (Paul Mitchell Salon Hair Care). I included their reviews on the front and back covers of that edition. I had also sent a copy of my manuscript to Margie Wagner-Clews of Empire Education Group, but it was during the time of their "National Competition and Hair Show," so I did not receive a review due to timing.

While I am grateful to all, I decided to change the cover beginning with the second edition of my book. Instead of reviews on that cover, I opted to include text that would help to extend the air of my book as being something of an "archaeological find." That is because hair braiding is a centuries old art that many from my generation will remember learning from their mothers, who learned the art of hair braiding from their mothers. In some ways I feel as though we have lost knowledge of that art. My book is autobiographical in nature, and represents my attempt to pass the knowledge of hair braiding and hair care that I learned from my mother and her family on to the next generation, so I wanted a cover that enforced the "ancientness" of hair braiding. With *Hair Braiding to Grow, Strengthen, and Lengthen Your Hair*, I have tried to maintain that concept of "ancientness" in the design of the cover.

I'd like to thank family and friends for their help with this work. And once again, I want to acknowledge and thank my readers, too. Thank you for forgiving any errors that I may have missed or created during the editing process. Your patronage is very much appreciated!

—Diana K. Mitchell

Message to My Readers

Thank you for purchasing my book! I pray that it blesses you.

My passion is to help women and children who have hair like mine (and be a help to women who may have adopted African American children) learn how to work with and properly care for the beautiful hair that God gave them. ***It is my desire to encourage people like me who may have felt less than beautiful in the past because they did not know how to properly care for their tightly curled hair.*** Even though my book is an instruction manual, it is autobiographical in nature; therefore, in my book I share my experiences with you, and what I have learned from my mother and her family about growing and taking care of tightly curled hair, such as my hair type, in order to help you learn how to grow your own hair to longer and healthier lengths.

In *Hair Braiding to Grow, Strengthen, and Lengthen Your Hair*, I share such things as how to wash your hair, for example, which may seem like an unnecessary step to include in a manual on how to braid hair. You may also think it unnecessary to be as repetitive as I have been with the instructions; however, not knowing the skill level of all of those who might purchase my book, I have written from an elementary perspective. The people I had in mind when I initially wrote this book were people who might not have someone to help them understand how to work with their hair type; primarily young ones who may be in the care of the state with no one to help them to understand their hair type, and mothers of other ethnicities whose children are part African American who have hair like mine. I have included seemingly unnecessary and repetitive instructions for them. But even if you think that you do not need help with learning how to wash your hair, please read those instructions anyway. One person shared with me that she had thought as much, too, but then she found I'd written something that was a help to her.

With that said, I'll share with you a little about my own hair type. In the past my hair has been anywhere from one-sixteenth of an inch long to as long as seventeen inches. It's usually one-sixteenth of an inch long after I cut out a *perm* that has gone bad. My perms usually "go bad" after I try to retouch my own hair. So, from that perspective, I want to encourage you to leave chemical treatments, and maybe even hair *pressing*, to the professionals, but learn how to take care of your natural hair for yourself.

My hair is thick and tightly curled. I describe my hair type as *tight curls*. At seventeen inches long, and wet, it can look like it's only two inches long. If I didn't comb it out and plait it before it dried, it would still look as though it were only two inches long after it dried. Please remember that this book reflects how I work with my hair. Even so, if your hair cannot be described as I just described my hair, it can still be braided, but use caution and experiment with the instructions in this book, particularly instructions that refer to adding *extensions* to the hair, to see if you need to adjust them to work with your hair type. In that regard, see bullet point 11 under "Things to Remember" in "A Brief Recap," chapter 5.

It is my prayer that you will find the information within the pages of this book a daily help to you in styling and learning to grow your natural hair. Once again, thank you for your patronage, but please don't keep this resource a secret. Please encourage others to buy my book, too. Your patronage is appreciated!

How to Read this Book

Disclaimer Information

Before you attempt to braid your hair, read this book thoroughly from cover to cover. As a matter of warning, for further advice or assistance, it is recommended that you visit a local professional skilled in the art of hair braiding and hair care, your physician, or a dermatologist.

    Any decision to experiment with or to put into use any information in this book is up to the individual/reader. The author, owner of the copyright, and publisher disclaim any liability for damage/loss, direct or indirect, as a probable cause or alleged cause of use of any information in this book, article, etcetera.

    The views expressed in this work are solely those of the author and do not necessarily reflect the views of the publisher, and the publisher hereby disclaims any responsibility for them.

    The author is not a licensed cosmetologist. This book reflects her experiences in learning how to braid and care for her own hair. If this book inspires you to braid someone's hair other than your own or your child's hair, please remember that in many states you must have a business license if you plan to charge someone for braiding their hair.

    No portion of this work may be reproduced/copied by any means without the publisher's/author's written permission.

Hair Braiding to Grow, Strengthen, and Lengthen Your Hair

Understanding Textual Notations

For your reading convenience, certain conventions have been instituted throughout this book:

Δ	This symbol indicates that the specified information should be noted as it relates to children and people with thin hair. When you see this symbol, remember to use less force on the hair. Although this symbol is used throughout the book, there are only four main headings, and one subheading, in the book where you will see this symbol used with a heading. Within these sections, this symbol applies to every paragraph under those headings, including any subheadings. Please see the "Glossary" for more information regarding this symbol.
NOTE:	This is used within paragraphs to highlight special information for you to note.
Take Note	This subheading term highlights several noteworthy paragraphs of information, which, usually, follow numbered lists.
Some Things to Think About	This heading appears at the end of each chapter with a brief summary of things to note and consider before moving on to the next chapter.
Italicized words	Words and terms that may not be familiar to the reader have been italicized, and have been included in the "Glossary." This does not apply to titles of books, magazines, movies, and words or phrases that have been italicized (obviously) for effect. Thus far four such items have been italicized (see page xii).

How to Read Instructional Information

For the reader's convenience, in "Step Two: Methods of Braiding and Extending Your Hair" there are two types of instructional

How to Read this Book

information: visual illustration groups, and text. The same heading title has been used for both text and illustration groups.

People who prefer visual-based learning will appreciate using the instructional illustrations that appear on the left-hand-side pages of this book. Illustrations have identifiers a, b, and c. Visual-based learners will use these identifiers to follow hair strands as they move through an illustration group.

For simplicity and ease of reading for text-based learners, corresponding text does not mention the illustration identifiers. Corresponding text appears on the right-hand-side pages of this book.

Numbers in an illustration group correspond to the numbered bullets in the text version of the illustration group. For example, the "African Braiding" illustration group begins with illustration #4, which corresponds to bullet point 4 in the instructional text on the opposite page. People who prefer both, text- and visual-based learning systems, will appreciate having both types of instructional information to learn from; taking in only what they need in order to understand the instructional group as a whole.

Editorial Changes

Second Edition Changes in *The Hair Braider's Secret Reference Manual*

In addition to a new cover, with this edition, I sought to increase self-awareness concerning African American hair. For example, to make it easier to identify the four headings in the book where the reader is encouraged to use less force on the hair, I added the "Δ" symbol to those headings in the table of contents.

Also with this edition, I changed the title of chapter 1 from "Introduction" to "Why Do You Want to Learn How to Braid Your Hair?" In that chapter, I added a commentary on African American hair and the 2009 documentary by Chris Rock, *Good Hair: Sit Back and Relax*.

Chapter 2, "Step One: The Preparation" was expanded to include a section on a particular type of hair breakage, and how to avoid it. In chapter 5, "A Brief Recap," I added to the text of "Maintaining a Healthy Head of Hair" in order to focus attention on what I believe to be the main reason why healthy hair may appear to not grow.

Chapter 6 was renamed from "Concluding Words" to "Some Things to Think About." Chapter 6 concludes the main instructional text of the book, so the new title was a better fit for the reader. The new title reflected the style of the book in that the same title was used, as noted on page xiv, at the end of each chapter. Likewise, before readers moved on to "Gallery of Hairstyles: Designs for Work, School, and Play," the new title was meant to encourage the reader to consider the points discussed in previous chapters.

Hairstyles were numbered in "Gallery of Hairstyles: Designs for Work, School, and Play," and a new hairstyle was added to this chapter. While other sections of the book were expanded upon, I decreased the size of "Your Personal Hair-care Diary" because I thought that it would be more effective with fewer pages. In addition, "Further Reading and Study" was reduced to two pages.

Changes in *Hair Braiding to Grow, Strengthen, and Lengthen Your Hair*

With this edition, I've taken the opportunity to change the title to better reflect the content of my book. As with the second edition, I've tried to also better word the text on the back cover in order to give people considering purchasing my book a little more information in regards to the text in my book.

New to this edition are mini quizzes titled "Quick Thought Check." I've scattered them throughout the book in order to help you retain information that you've read. They can be located via the "Table of Contents" and by using the "Index." They're meant to be fun, so don't stress. In addition, I've added snippets titled **"HOMEWORK"** that are meant to slow you down so that you take a moment or two to take in what you are doing with your hair. These can be located in the book via the "Index."

Chapter 1, "Why Do You Want to Learn How to Braid Your Hair?" has been renamed "Understanding My African Hair." In addition, the subsection within that chapter titled "Why Do We Braid Our Hair" has been expanded and renamed "Becoming 'Hair' Conscious." In chapter 4, "Step Three: Braid Care," a section titled "The Afro" has been added.

Chapter 6 has been renamed from "Some Things to Think About" to "A Bald-Headed Woman" because this title better reflects the importance of hair to the individual. A hairstyle has been removed from the "Gallery of Hairstyles: Designs for Work, School, and Play," chapter 7, because I decided that it would work better as a hairstyle for loose hair rather than as a braided hairstyle. Chapter 8, "Your Personal Hair-care Diary," has been incorporated into chapter 7 as a subheading of that chapter, and titled "Your Personal Hair-Care Diary." I've increased the size of that section with this edition in order to give my readers more room for taking notes. The "Glossary of Terms" has been renamed simply "Glossary." There were to be two glossaries with the first edition, one for hairstyles and one for terms. I decided against having a hairstyle glossary with the first edition because, in the end, I decided that I wanted the focus of the book to remain on learning how to braid the hair in order to grow it. I kept the title "Glossary of Terms" simply because I liked it. Now that title just seems redundant.

A major change with this edition has been to remove religious references, especially those to specific organizations. Re-reading what I'd written in previous editions, I decided that some of what I'd written concerning God seemed like I'd forced it into fitting my book. Hence my correcting that issue with this edition of my book. I have, however, left in my experiences with God that revolved around hair, especially if I felt those experiences might be of help to some of you all. In addition, while this is not a theological, or scholarly, work, I feel that if God allowed me to have such experiences, then they are important to note in this work.

As with the previous editions, what hasn't changed with this edition is my commitment to give you the best book that I can, which is a book that you will, it is hoped, want to keep and perhaps pass down to your descendants.

Hair Braiding to Grow, Strengthen, and Lengthen Your Hair

Quick Thought Check #1

1. What does this "Δ" symbol mean?
2. Italicized words in this manual indicate the author's emphasis on a particular word as someone might do when speaking during a conversation.
   A. True
   B. False

QTC #1 Answers

1. Please see pages xiv, and 125 for the answer to this question.
2. The answer to this question is "B," false. Please see page xiv.

Chapter 1
| Understanding My African Hair

When I was growing up, my mother told me that you have to train your hair in order for it to grow. In other words, growing our African American hair is something that we have to learn how to do.

I don't think that I really understood what that meant until I decided to have my hair braided with extensions one day. Money was tight back then, but I loved the look so much that I decided to braid my hair every week myself because I couldn't afford to pay someone else to do it for me on a weekly basis. I braided my hair every week for one and a half years. Ever since that time, my hair has grown like wildfire.

When I looked around me back then, I could see that there was—and there still is today—a need for information such as is contained within the pages of this book, and so I began to write this book. I completed this work years ago and put it on a shelf.

Even though I could see the need, I didn't feel like it was time to publish my work back then. For example, I was friends with a Latina in Virginia, who was married to a black man. They had a beautiful child together. I remember one day my friend telling me that she didn't know how to care for her child's hair. She also told me that not even her mother really knew how to care for her daughter's hair. Although I could see my friend's need, I still did not feel that it was time to publish this work.

Now is the time. And, according to an analysis of the

United States Census Bureau, "Table MS-3. Interracial Married Couples: 1980 to 2002," same-race marriages decreased from 1980 to 2002, while interracial marriages increased. I think it likely that more biracial African American children are being born to women who need help learning how to care for their children's hair. Although my book is written with African Americans in mind, I hope members from every ethnicity, male and female, will purchase my book and enjoy reading it as they learn how to braid and care for their hair and their children's hair.

Becoming "Hair Conscious"

I learned how to plait hair out of necessity. My mother would always plait our hair each morning before we left for school. I remember one morning insisting on doing my hair myself. When I finally admitted that I couldn't do it myself, and that I needed help, it was too late because my sister and I had to leave for school, and my mother had to leave for an appointment. I had to settle for a makeshift hairstyle that morning that I somehow threw together. It looked horrible. I think that is when I became conscious of my hair, and decided to learn how to plait my own hair.

I can't remember exactly when I learned how to braid hair, but once I learned how to plait my hair, I couldn't stay away from the mirror, and I wanted to learn everything that I could about hair. My mother had purchased us a set of the *World Book Encyclopedia* and I nearly wore the spine print off of the *H* volume because I would read the article on hair over and over again. I also remember learning terms from my mother, her sisters, and other relatives such as *overhand plaiting*, *underhand plaiting*, and *cornrows*. However, centuries old, braiding is a unique method of styling the hair that has been passed down from generation to generation. So, my mother and her sisters did not invent these terms or techniques, and neither did I. They learned them from their mother, and other relatives, and passed that knowledge down to me. This is the knowledge that I am passing on to you.

The home stylist who originally braided my hair with extensions used a common over-and-go type of method to add extensions to my hair. Although she did a good job, it was obvious that I was wearing hair extensions and I preferred a more natural look, so I began to experiment. The methods that you will learn in this book to extend your braided styles are the results of my experiments; they are what I have learned through trial and error and, when my hair was too short to hold extensions, necessity.

    I've thus far literally used the terms "braids" and "cornrows," interchangeably, but which is the correct term to use when braiding hair? This can be confusing, but the other day, I remembered a conversation that I had with one of my relatives when I was a child. The difference between the two hairstyles confused me because I couldn't see a difference. I had wondered why "they" called braids "cornrows." I was informed "because they look like cornrows."

    So I came to understand that whichever term you used depended on where you lived. In other words, the terms "to braid" and "to cornrow" were two terms that referred to one particular hairstyling method known today as African braiding. Northerners seemed to use the term "cornrows," while southerners used the term "braids." Northerners "put cornrows in," while southerners "got their hair braided." Northerners "cornrowed," while southerners "braided" their hair. I also noticed that we tend to refer to plaits as braids, too. So, following that tradition, in this manual, *braiding* is the term that we will use occasionally to refer to plaits, and all braided hairstyle types. When specific terminology is not used (i.e. African braids, French braids, etc.), then any reference to "braids" applies to all braided hairstyle types.

Hair and Discrimination in the Workplace

Speaking of terminology and the way we use words, at this point I would like to share with you an issue involving hair consciousness that affects African Americans in general, as opposed to sharing with you an experience that is uniquely my own. After the second edition of my book, I began to research information for a bookmark to complement it. This research lead me to the stories of Melba Tolliver, Renee Rogers, and Cheryl Tatum.

    In 1971, Tolliver nearly lost her job as an ABC news affiliate for wearing an Afro while covering the wedding of President Nixon's daughter, Tricia Nixon. Rogers, an American Airlines ticket agent was fired from her job in 1981 for wearing braids to work; she eventually lost the lawsuit she brought against the airline. Tatum likewise was fired from her part-time cashier's job at a Hyatt Hotel in 1987 because she refused to change her braided hairstyle. Tatum took her case to the Equal Employment Opportunity Commission, and eventually won her suit against Hyatt.

Almost 50 years after Tolliver stood up for herself, women of African descent in the United States still face hostile attitudes and subtle racism in the workplace simply for wearing their natural hair styled in ways that work best for their hair types. A paper written in 2018 by Gail Dawson and Katherine Karl of the University of Tennessee at Chattanooga, and published in the *Journal of Business Diversity*, strongly demonstrates this peril, which is faced by many African American women on a daily basis. Dawson and Karl review court cases, including that of Rogers' to make their point in their paper, "I am not my Hair, or am I? Examining Hair Choices of Black Female Executives."

While the focus of my book is not a legal review of cases fought on behalf of defending the right of African American women and men to style their hair in ways not ultimately harmful to themselves, I cannot leave this section without mentioning the first statewide law in the United States that protects African Americans from hair discrimination: The CROWN Act, of July 2019, championed by California state Sen. Holly Mitchell, signed into California law by Gov. Gavin Newsom on Wednesday, July 3, 2019, and published in *California Legislative Counsel's Digest* on July 4, 2019. Likewise, the "Anti-Black racism" guidelines passed by the New York City Commission on Human Rights in February 2019, make it illegal to discriminate against "natural hair or hairstyles associated with Black people." These documents, and past lawsuits, represent a need in the workplace to better protect African Americans from employers who fail to protect their rights to advancement by allowing, or fostering environments that allow, destructive comments made by their direct managers and fellow employees concerning their hair, a unique cultural identifier, to go unpunished.

Our beliefs make up who we are; therefore, it should be taken seriously whenever someone who has the power to promote the individual makes destructive comments in the workplace. Such comments have nothing to do with the fact that they are not nice comments, but with their power to destroy the individual by decreasing their value in the eyes of others, which in turn may affect their ability to provide for themselves and their families.

Based on the history of slavery, such comments should especially be taken seriously in the workplace because they may consciously (or unconsciously) diminish the worth of an entire group of people, and their ability to economically advance, by what can be described as *subtile racism against their God-given hair types*. We are born with our hair types, they are not self-assigned.

In addition, African American hair types are unique, and distinguishable by how they must be cared for, as is evidenced by styling tools that have been developed specifically for combing African hair types, such as, for example, the pick. No other ethnicity among the human race has to use specially designed combing instruments to comb and style their hair.

Your Hair Is Your Crown

Moving the focus back to myself, I remember with fondness something else that my mother told me and my sister growing up, and that is that "your hair is your ***crown***." This is another saying regarding hair from my mother that I wasn't exactly sure about. While editing my book for this edition, I came across a biblical scripture that helped to clarify the matter for me: Jeremiah 2:16, which reads "Moreover, the people of Memphis and Tahpanhes have broken the crown of your head." Some scholars believe that this verse might refer to a woman's hair, as the NRSV note states.

I had originally thought that my mother was making a reference to an African proverb, but when I think back to my grandmother (my mother's mother, who came from "some praying people"), a biblical reference makes sense, too. Of course, as a descendant of American slaves, it could also refer to an African proverb. I recently had the opportunity to learn from an older woman that when she asked God how to grow her hair, God's reply to her was that she should wear her hair on top of her head. That style makes the hair look like a crown. When my hair isn't in braids, I have found that wearing my hair up on top of my head forces me, for the most part, to keep my hands out of my hair during the day, protecting my hair from the most destructive force: my hands.

Either way, wearing your hair up or down, how you regard

your hair is important. Have you ever missed an outing because your hair didn't look right? Or, to use the term coined by Philip Kingsley, have you ever had a "bad hair day" (Kingsley 2014, 20)? There is no doubt about it, hair is a source of self-esteem, and because it is, we owe it to ourselves to develop a healthy sense of hair-esteem, and take a good look at how we treat our crown (please make sure you read chapter 6, "A Bald-Headed Woman"), and how we allow it to be treated by others.

Brief Reflection on African American Hair and Braiding

In regards to self-esteem and hair, my first exposure to braids as a hairstyle of distinction and cultural pride came with a January 1979 *Ebony* magazine article on Cicely Tyson. I remember seeing her on the cover and thinking that she was *beauty defined*—like my mother—and as such to be emulated. She made braids look so elegant. Cicely Tyson starred in roles that uplifted, exemplified the mental strength of, and brought dignity to, African American women. She was interesting also because she did not play stereotypical roles.

I still hold this actress in high regard. When I saw her on the cover of *Ebony* with her hair in braids, I remember thinking that if she could wear her hair like that, then it was okay for me to wear mine in braids, too. Today that is an odd thought to me, but back then the African American community was (and I think to a large degree still is) in the process of defining itself as a cultural group, post-slavery.

At the time of the January 1979 *Ebony* article, braids as a hairstyle to complement business dress, or as a social hairstyle, were frowned upon. It took someone with self-confidence to wear them in any business or social setting. I am so thankful that Cicely Tyson, a high-profile actress, was able to be herself and use her celebrity to help African Americans feel comfortable styling their God-given hair for any business or social setting in ways better suited to their unique hair type.

While researching the January 1979 *Ebony* cover to make sure that I had the correct date, I discovered that Cicely Tyson had also appeared, wearing what looks to me to be nonextended braids, on the cover of the March 15, 1973 issue of *Jet* magazine. In addition, I've discovered that the April 1975 cover of *Ebony* is also a cover to note. Campus queens in this issue wear every hairstyle imaginable among African Americans. On the cover, each wears a different hairstyle: big, and small, *Afros*; pressed hair; and one, Janell Marie Richards, wears her hair in beautiful nonextended braids.

After the January 1979 Tyson article in *Ebony*, I remember seeing an article in *Essence* magazine written by Kariamu Welsh that inspired me, too. The article—in the May 1980 anniversary issue titled "Black Girls Can Shake Their Hair Now!"—was a radical, albeit brief, look at the history of the braided hairstyle. A beautiful Julie Woodson wearing her hair braided on that *Essence* cover was as ground-breaking as the *Ebony* cover of Cicely Tyson wearing her hair in braids. Though the article uplifts and encourages the reader, the seven words that made up the title of that 1980 *Essence* magazine article, and the exclamation point, revealed more than any book ever could about how African American women regarded their specific hair type in comparison to other ethnic hair types.

Other inspirations for me include gospel singer and radio talk show host Yolanda Adams, and Valerie Simpson of the singing duo "Ashford and Simpson" (Nickolas "Nick" Ashford and Valerie Simpson). These women, like Cicely Tyson, showed us a different way to wear, and think about braids—as an elegant hairstyle to be worn with dignity.

After Tyson's appearance on the *Ebony* cover, I remember seeing actress Bo Derek in beaded braids in a promotion for the October 1979 movie *10*. Her appearance in that movie, wearing braids, popularized the hairstyle to the general public. Derek's beaded braids were reminiscent of the Fulani, and, because of how they were decorated, they also reminded me of a similar type of beaded braids hairstyle worn by "Peaches" of the "Peaches and Herb" singing duo (Linda Green and Herb "Fame" Feemster). "Peaches and Herb" grace the cover of the June 1979 edition of *Ebony*, while their story is chronicled on the pages within by Lynn Norment. Singer Patrice Rushen also wore beaded braids for a time. The beaded braids looks Rushen wore on her 1979 *Pizzazz*, and 1982 *Straight from the Heart* album covers are iconic.

Thirty years later, comedian Chris Rock's 2009 documentary, *Good Hair: Sit Back and Relax*, revealed an attitude held by some African Americans toward their own hair that is reminiscent of like attitudes held by African Americans during the 1940s. Rock produced the documentary because one of his daughters asked him one day why she didn't have good hair.

What is interesting to me as an African American is that the comments made by some of the people interviewed for Rock's 2009 documentary reflect similar comments made by Malcolm X about hair in chapter 3, "'Homeboy',' of his 1964 autobiography, *The Autobiography of Malcolm X: As Told to Alex Haley*.

Despite the passage of time, Rock's documentary and Malcolm X's comments reveal a struggle to accept, within the general African American community, African American hair types. This, while we have been busy seeking legislation against discrimination, reveals to me that we haven't focused enough on ourselves, but on, and rightly so, the necessity of fighting the outward foe of discrimination. From the Malcolm X/Chris Rock perspective, if in this day and age we are still struggling to accept our own hair types, I have to ask two rhetorical questions: **Does the rest of the world benefit from that struggle, financially or otherwise? If so, how?**

The elders of my family have noted to me that in post-slavery America, African Americans experienced a very real, and intense, need to present themselves to the majority population, who controlled economic resources, as being physically similar to that population. This included mimicking hairstyles of that population. In doing so, many African Americans hoped to be accepted as being similar to that population so that they could earn a living to support themselves and their families. Ironically, they did this hoping to avoid being discriminated against.

There still exists a struggle to accept African hair types among the general population and African Americans. As one non-African American beauty store clerk noted to me one day, the majority of the people who share my hair type seem to have short hair, unlike myself at the time—and I'll add to her comment—that they struggle to accept because of the difficulty associated with maintaining it, and because of how it is viewed by the larger society. Rock's documentary reveals the need to be deliberate in moving past these vestiges of slavery. The CROWN Act, and the New York City law that preceded it, are a start. We have to become more deliberate in our own self-acceptance, even as others try to help us lose, via subtile racism, the economic ground of self-sufficiency that we have gained. I want to encourage you to take the time to deliberately look in the mirror and look at the beauty that God placed in our African hair types, and encourage yourself. Every time you pass a mirror, look at your reflection and deliberately say to yourself: *My permed/ natural hair is gorgeous, I love my hair, it is magnificently made, like me, by God!* (Here I make reference to Psalm 139:13-14 in the Bible.)

Even though Rock's documentary reveals as being still alive today a centuries old love/hate relationship with our hair, we have witnessed within the past few decades the braided hairstyle progress from an artistic, cultural statement to a practical hairstyle for a busy lifestyle. Today, women and men from all walks of life enjoy creative and simplistic braided styles for a variety of reasons: cultural; as a way to grow hair longer; as a resting phase for damaged hair; as a beautification or aesthetic grooming tool like makeup, earrings, or fingernail polish; as a practical answer to aid a demanding business schedule; and, obviously, simply because the wearer chooses to style her/his hair in braided styles.

Whatever your reasons are for choosing this method of styling your hair, the best way to learn how to braid is to have the attitude that you are willing to take the time and experiment with your hair so that you can get to know *your* hair. I have learned that hair growth can be a by-product of hair braiding, but to maintain hair growth, you must be willing to make changes to how you care for your hair, based on your experiments.

Before you learn how to braid hair, you should know how to plait hair. This book has been written from the perspective that the reader knows how to plait hair, which is the basis of all braided styles. However, for those who do not know how to plait hair, a section on how to plait hair has been included following the sections on African braiding and French braiding. The section on plaiting the hair acts to clarify any remaining questions concerning the difference between African braiding and French braiding.

After having worn my hair braided in one form or another, on and off, all of my life, I have found that there are three important steps to braiding that you should follow in attempting to obtain, or maintain, a healthy head of hair. These steps are presented in detail in the following chapters. To help you prepare for them, following is a list of materials that you will need to use in each of these chapters.

Materials You Will Need

Step One (for use with "Step One: The Preparation"):
1. *Fiber*
2. Shampoo, wash-out conditioner, leave-in conditioner
3. Hanger and clothespin
4. Combs—wide-toothed or a seamless plastic Afro pick (my preference) for combing the hair, fine-toothed for parting the hair while braiding
5. Hair scissors (also known as shears)
6. Mirrors, stationary and handheld (use the handheld one in conjunction with a stationary dresser mirror for a view of the sides and back of your head)
7. Satin *scrunchies* to hold the hair out of the way
8. Optional: hair dryer, hair grease/oil

Step Two (for use with "Step Two: Methods of Braiding and Extending Your Hair"):
1. Fiber from "Step One" above
2. Fine-toothed comb
3. Mirrors
4. Hair scissors
5. Bobby pins and scrunchies
6. Optional: rubber bands

Step Three (for use with "Step Three: Braid Care"):
1. Satin hair scarf/stocking cap
2. Shampoo, wash-out conditioner, leave-in conditioner
3. Fresh fiber, or re-use fiber from "Step Two" above
4. Hair scissors
5. Bobby pins and scrunchies
6. Optional: hair grease/oil, rubber bands, hair dryer, pick, wide-toothed comb, mirrors, fresh fiber, a ball-tipped *seam ripper* with a safety cover, clippers, and a boar-bristle brush
   Δ   Use a soft brush for a child's/thin hair, a hard one for tightly curled adult hair

Some Things to Think About

Loving your hair as God made it, and wearing it permed or natural is one thing. If it's not growing as you would like for it to grow, whether it is permed or natural, is another thing. If your hair is not growing, it may be because of something you are doing to it, it may have reached its peak length, or there could be something medically wrong and you may want to consult a physician.

Do you want your hair to grow longer? Your answer determines what you will get out of my book. I had to admit to myself when I started to braid my own hair—with extensions—that I wanted long hair. For me, an African American woman with short hair at the time that most of my cultural group would describe as bad, *kinky* hair, that was not an easy declaration to make to myself. But I'm so glad that I made that declaration because I firmly believe that you can't fix anything if you don't, or won't, admit that it's broken, and my hair seemed "broken" to me. It didn't seem to grow, and there was nothing medically wrong. I've since discovered that my hair wasn't "broken." The way I was caring for it was the problem.

My hair didn't grow long until I learned, from braiding it, how to work with it and "train" it to grow. When the women of my mother's day said that you have to train your hair, I think that what they were really saying is that you have to train yourself on how to comb and care for your hair so as not to impede its growth. If I'm correct about that, then I am a testament that they were right. When I started to braid my hair, there were all sorts of myths floating around that braiding your hair would cause baldness. I wanted to make sure that braiding my hair did not leave me bald, so I took pains to make sure that my hair was in the best shape that it could be in while it was braided. *And even though I only occasionally wear my hair in braids these days, it continues to grow like wildfire because of the lessons I learned while wearing it braided.*

I want to pass those lessons on to you, my reader. And whether your hair is long now, or short, I pray you are able to glean something good from my book that will be of use to you long after you've finished the final chapter. Now, with the "Materials You Will Need" list in hand, you are ready to begin your journey in learning to braid with chapter 2, "Step One: The Preparation."

Quick Thought Check #2

1. Depending on context, the term "braids" in this manual may refer to:
   A. African braids
   B. French braids
   C. Plaits
   D. All of the above
   E. None of the above

2. Chris Rock and Malcolm X have nothing in common.
   A. True
   B. False

3. The author's hair can be defined as:
   A. Loose Curls
   B. Tight Curls
   C. Body Straight
   D. Bone Straight
   E. Loose or Tight Waves

4. Braids should not be worn in a business setting.
   A. True
   B. False

5. Do you want your hair to grow longer?
   A. Yes
   B. I'm not vain
   C. A and B above
   D. I'm not sure, I don't want to sound vain

QTC #2 Answers

1. The correct answer is "D," all of the above. Please see page 21.
2. False. Please see page 26.
3. "B" is the correct answer. Please see page xii.
4. False. Please see page 27.
5. The answer to this question depends on you. I selected answer "C" for my response. Please see page 29.

Chapter 2
| Step One: The Preparation

Your first question is probably: What on earth am I going to do with that laundry list of ingredients at the end of the previous chapter? The answer to that question is spread throughout this book, and you most likely will use everything on that list. Next, if you plan to extend your braided style, you're probably wondering where to obtain the false hair that you will need. It may be purchased from beauty supply stores, wig shops, variety stores, or flea markets/swap meets.

The two types of hair used in extension braiding are synthetic and human hair. In learning to braid, I recommend using the synthetic hair because it is less expensive than human hair. You should plan to buy at least four packages of the synthetic hair for braids that are to be at least midway down your back. For longer braids, you should plan to buy twice as much synthetic hair. The first time that you braid your hair with extensions, it's better to have too much and not need it, than to have too little and then have to run out to the store—halfway through the braiding process—to buy more.

From this point forward we will call both synthetic and human hair *fiber*. Directions in this book will generally refer to synthetic fiber, which is easier to work with when learning how to braid hair.

Δ Another question that you may have before you begin learning how to braid hair is: Should I even use extensions in my hair? I believe that if your hair is thin, or if you are braiding a child's hair, then you should not use extensions. This is because the temptation when braiding thin hair, or a child's hair, is to use more fiber with the hair than necessary, which may cause the natural hair to break off. But continue reading so that you will understand how to use extensions. Once you understand what is involved, then should you choose to, you'll be in a better position to use extensions on thin hair, or on a child's hair.

Preparing the Fiber

You will eventually develop your own method for washing fiber. In the meantime, you may want to use the following steps to prepare the fiber for your hair.

1. One or two days before you plan to braid your hair, shampoo and condition *(wash)* the fiber. To do this, remove the fiber from its plastic wrap, but do not remove the bindings. **NOTE:** If the fiber does not look like a large plait, remove the rubber band binding at the bottom *(free end)* and loosely plait the fiber (see pages 58-59 if you do not know how to plait hair yet); replace the rubber band when you finish.
2. Wet the fiber thoroughly, pour a small amount of shampoo along its length, and work up a lather. To do this, hold the fiber at the top *(bound end)* and open and close your free hand along the length of it until you reach the free end. Do this several times, and gently twist and wring the fiber, as you would if you were trying to get a stain out of a blouse or other article of clothing.
3. Once you have worked up a good lather, rinse the fiber using the same method used to work the shampoo through. Follow this method to condition the fiber, too.
4. After the final rinse, utilize a hanger and clothespin and hang the fiber indoors to dry. To do this, cut the rubber band binding off the free end only. Unplait the fiber, and hang one of the three strands over the hanger; secure with the clothespin. Do not remove the rubber band binding of the bound end.

Take Note

It is very important that you wash the fiber before using it in your real hair. This cleanses it by removing most manufacturing dust particles and debris. Not washing this dust and debris from the fiber could cause unbearable itching once the fiber has been braided into the real hair. If you like, you may use a hair dryer to shorten the drying time of the fiber. Do not, however, use a comb attachment.

Preparing Your Hair

First, wash your combs and brushes with the same shampoo and leave-in conditioner (or wash-out conditioner) that you will be using on your hair. As you will do with your hair, do not rinse the leave-in conditioner from your comb or brush. Use a towel to remove any excess leave-in conditioner from your comb and brush.

If you are using a hair dryer to speed the drying time of the fiber, and will be blow-drying your own hair, stop when the fiber is almost completely dry, and wash and dry your own hair. After washing your hair use a towel to blot excess water. Be aware that you will be combing your hair while it is still wet. **NOTE:** Do not comb dry hair before washing it because that only serves to break your hair off.

Following is how I wash my hair. Until you discover the best way to wash your own hair, you may want to use the following routine.

1. I've found that the best way to wash my hair (natural or *permed*) is to wash it in the shower. If you don't have a shower, try using a shower attachment in the bathtub. The idea is to keep your hair in a vertical position as you wash it, and not bunch it up. If you can keep it in a vertical position, you will have fewer tangles to comb out later.
2. Δ Thoroughly wet your hair and pour a handful of shampoo into your hands; rub it over your head, patting it into your scalp. Once the shampoo begins to lather in your hair, use a gentle side-to-side scratching motion on your scalp to help remove any *buildup*. Use the gentle scratching motion all over your scalp until it feels clean. Finger-part your hair into halves and gently cleanse one half by opening and closing your hands down the length of it; do the other half the same way. **NOTE:** Pay attention to the color of the shampoo as you work it through your hair. If it isn't white, you probably need to repeat this step after doing step 3. If your hair is too short

to finger-part into halves, finger-part it into smaller sections, or simply continue to gently press the lather into your scalp using the patting motion you used to distribute the shampoo throughout your hair.
3. Rinse the shampoo from your hair by gently patting your scalp and opening and closing your hands down the length of your hair as the water flows through it.
4. If you are using a wash-out conditioner, use the same motions that you used to shampoo your hair—pat your scalp, and open and close your hands down the length of your hair—to cover your hair with the conditioner and then rinse it from your hair.
5. Towel-dry your hair by wrapping a towel around your head and gently pressing it into your scalp; let it sit on your head for a few minutes so that excess water is absorbed into the towel.
   Δ A word of caution: Never scrub your scalp with a towel because the friction from the scrubbing may break off hairs, especially along your *hairline*.
6. If you use grease or oil on your scalp, you may want to begin now to *wean* yourself from using these product types directly on your scalp. Place a small amount of oil/grease/leave-in conditioner in the palm of your hand, about the size of an acorn, for example, if your hair is shoulder length. If you are using a leave-in conditioner, which (to me) is better for your hair, you may use more to cover your hair. Gently rub it over approximately one-fourth of your hair, from the ends to just within one-eighth inch of your scalp. Do the rest of your hair.
7. Now begin sectioning your hair with a wide-tooth comb. Make a part down the center of your scalp, from the front to the back of your head. When you run into resistance, remove the comb, and using your fingers, gently separate the hair through the resistance to the ends. Continue to part through to the back.
8. Divide one of the two halves in half, from the top of your head down to your ear. Secure one half out of your way, and detangle the other section by combing your hair from the ends up to the scalp. (For this, I use a smooth Afro pick with no jagged edges.

NOTE: My hair sits up and away from my scalp. An Afro pick can reach down through the depths of my hair so that I am combing all hairs in a section at one time. An Afro comb, on the other hand, would only allow me to comb the "top" hairs, leaving the hairs not visible still tangled.) When you run into resistance, use your fingers to separate the hairs in the tangle, then continue detangling. It also helps to wet the pick (not your hair) when you run into resistance, and then use it to comb your hair. Plait this hair and then go on to the next section. For short hair, it may be necessary to divide the subsections into smaller sections. If your hair is three to four inches past your shoulders, it will be easier to comb if you gently pull it out to its full length and hold it near the ends in your fist. You will be opening and closing your fist as you comb your hair. Holding longer hair in your fist as you comb it will help you to maintain control over your hair. Exercising that control may help decrease breakage. Δ If your hair is long enough to where you can hold it in your fist as you comb it, continue to comb it gently, stopping to use your fingers to separate hairs that tangle when you need to do so. Never force a comb through your hair.

9. The best way to dry your hair is naturally. If you must use a hair dryer to save time, use it on a low, cool setting. When using a hair dryer, the less heat the better, particularly if your ends are damaged, or if your hair is permed. If your hair dryer has a comb attachment, you may want to begin at the roots, combing through to the ends of your already detangled hair. Each time you run into resistance, lift the dryer from your hair and gently comb the remaining hair. It helps to restart slightly, approximately one-eighth inch to one-fourth inch below the resistance. Continue combing until you run into more resistance. This time try restarting midway along the length of hair already blown dry. Replait this hair and go on to the next section.

10. Once all sections are dry, unplait one section and *trim* split ends, if necessary, using a sharp pair of hair scissors. Replait and do the remaining sections.

11. You are now ready to part out the *main sections* of your

chosen style. This may be accomplished in one of two ways: (1) Unplait all sections and simply repart according to the main sections of your chosen style; or (2) Unplait the front two sections and repart the hair according to the main sections of your chosen style. Replait this new section, then go on to the next section and do the same, including unplaited hair from the previous section.

Take Note
Remember to never force a comb through your hair. If your hair is dry and badly tangled, try washing it and trimming your ends before combing it.

Δ If your hair type is like mine, tight curls, never pull it too tightly to the back, for example, and secure it when it is wet with any type of binding because, as your hair dries, it will most likely tighten over your scalp even more. Over the years, this may cause hair loss. More immediately, it will probably cause a bad headache that may send you running to your doctor to make sure that you are not physically ill. Instead, allow any wet hair pulled to the back into a binding to have some slack between the binding and your scalp.

Δ Preventing Hairline Breakage

I want to stop here and ask you to take special notice of your *line areas*. In the past, whenever my hair was permed, I'd eventually notice a lot of breakage along my *neckline*, and in as far as two inches from my neckline. I had thought that the breakage had something to do with the perms, but after the first publication of this work, I started to notice similar breakage—on my unpermed, natural hair. I didn't have to wonder where the damage was coming from as no one other than myself had worked on my hair up unto that point.

To prevent this type of hair breakage, I've learned to use one hand to smooth up and hold (*SUAH, "Smooth Up and Hold"*) loose hairs out of the way of my wash cloth and towel—even if I am wearing a shower cap I check that I haven't left out any loose hairs. I've found that if I don't do this when I wash the back of my neck or dry it with a towel, then the hairs near my neckline (even hairs as far away as two inches in from my neckline) eventually break off at the point where they are getting caught between the back of my neck, and the friction created from the back and forth rubbing motion that

I use with my wash cloth and towel. NOTE: Although the neckline area is the area where I've noticed the most damage from this type of breakage, I've learned that the same holds true for other line areas.

The next time you wash and dry the back of your neck (or any line area) stop and take note to see if you're catching some of your loose hairs between the back of your neck, and your wash cloth and towel. I call this a *HALT* (*"Hair and Lines Test"*). Since I've started doing HALTs and SUAHs, I've noticed that breakage along my line areas has decreased significantly.

Help your hairstylist at the salon, and SUAH there, too. For example, SUAH before the stylist places a towel around your shoulders in preparation to wash your hair.

Some Things to Think About

In this chapter I have tried to stress the importance of preparing your hair and the fiber for the braiding process. We've also stopped to take a look at a particular type of hair breakage.

The processes that I've noted in this book are how I treat my hair. If you're not sure how to wash and comb your hair, try the processes I've written here in this chapter. As you learn how to work with your hair, try reversing these processes—if a process states to begin combing at the ends, try reversing the process on your hair, and instead begin combing your hair from the roots out. In this instance, ***the objective is to experiment*** in order to observe the differences between combing from the roots and combing from the ends. If your hair is short and you do not notice a difference, keep testing this out. As your hair grows, you should begin to notice a big difference between combing your hair out from the roots, and combing it out from the ends of your hair.

I encourage you to experiment with your hair as described above in order for you to begin to discover for yourself what works for you in terms of growing your hair, and what does not work for you. Experimentation is the only way that you will get to know your hair type, learn how to work with your hair type, and learn how you would like for others to work with your hair type. With the knowledge in this chapter, you are off to a good start and are now ready to braid your hair using one of the methods in the next chapter, "Step Two: Methods of Braiding and Extending Your Hair."

Quick Thought Check #3

1. SUAH means:
    A. Stand Up And Holla
    B. Sit Up and Hear
    C. Smooth Up and Hold
    D. Speak Up At the Hairstylist's (for example, when your hairstylist tugs too hard on your hair)

2. HALT means:
    A. Have A Long Talk (with your hairstylist, for example)
    B. Hair and Lunch Time
    C. Hair and Lines Test
    D. Have and Love Too

3. In this manual "fiber" refers to:
    A. Eating right
    B. Rope
    C. Synthetic hair
    D. Human hair
    E. C and D above
    F. A and C above

4. False hair should be used:
    A. Within 30 days after purchase
    B. After it has been washed
    C. Immediately after purchase
    D. Within two weeks after purchase

5. Tightly secure wet hair with a scrunchie.
    A. True
    B. False

QTC #3 Answers

1. "C" is the correct answer. SUAH is an acronym that stands for Smooth Up and Hold. Please see page 36.
2. HALT is an acronym that stands for Hair and Lines Test. "C" is the correct answer. Please see page 37.
2. The answer is "E," both "C" and "D" are correct. Please see page 31.
4. The correct answer is "B," after it has been washed. Please see pages 32-33.
5. "B," false, is the correct answer. Please see page 36.

Chapter 3
| *Step Two: Methods of Braiding and Extending Your Hair*

WARNING!! Please forgive my dramatics! I just wanted to make sure that I got your attention, and I knew that you would **STOP!** when you saw that word in that font style. Here's what I wanted to say to you: If you begin reading my book from here, or skip to the pages that instruct you on how to braid your hair and read them first, this book will profit you nothing. If you haven't, please read my book from the beginning. I want you to get the most out of your purchase. In addition to that, the text that precedes this chapter prepares you for this chapter, and it gives you a firm foundation in learning how to use *Hair Braiding to Grow, Strengthen, and Lengthen Your Hair*. That's all, normal reading may now commence, again, and thanks for stopping to read this paragraph!

~~~~~~~~~~~~~

In "Step One: The Preparation," you parted your hair according to the main sections of your chosen hairstyle. Now select a section with which to work.

   Example: Pretend that your hair has been sectioned, and plaited, in quarters with two sections in the front, and two horizontal divisions in the back of your head. Starting at the back of your head, unplait the bottom section and vertically part it slightly off center. This will be your *main part*. The main part determines the direction the braids are to lay in relation to the wearers' shoulders: horizontal, diagonal, or perpendicular.

Replait one side. Part the loose side again, parallel to the first part. Bobby pin, use a scrunchie, or plait the rest of the hair to the side out of your way. You now have a thin, or thick if you like, *slice* of hair with which to work.

Why are we starting at the back of your head? I advocate starting at the back because it is easier to control the braiding process when learning how to braid. Plus, it keeps you from looking at what you are doing, which can interfere with what you are trying to learn how to do in so far as learning how to braid is concerned. Also, if you are just learning how to braid your child's hair, the middle back area of the head is probably the least sensitive area on the scalp. At least it is for me, and I have a very sensitive scalp.

Δ Before you begin braiding your hair, please note that as you complete a braid, you should do a quick check, to see if you have braided your hair too close to your scalp (*too tight*), by smiling and nodding your head up and down and from side to side. If you feel pain doing any of these movements, you have braided your hair too tight and should rebraid wherever you feel pain in order to avoid ***possibly irreversible hair loss***.

As you learn the different braiding techniques, practice braiding sections of hair at a time. To keep your braids neat looking, braid each section from left to right if you're right-handed; from right to left if you are left-handed.

You are now ready to learn how to African braid your hair. Did I hear someone say woohoo!?

Quick Thought Check #4

1. You should braid your hair as tight as possible so that it stays neat as long as possible.
    A. True
    B. False

2. You should braid your hair as tight as possible in order to keep fiber from falling out.
    A. True
    B. False

3. The middle back of the head is the least sensitive area on the scalp.
    A. Yes
    B. No
    C. Maybe

4. Braiding hair too close to the scalp is braiding the hair too tight, and this may eventually cause irreversible hair loss.
    A. True
    B. False

5. If you only brought this book to learn how to braid hair, you should skip to the pages that instruct on how to do that.
    A. True
    B. False

QTC #4 Answers

1. False. Braiding the hair too tight can eventually cause the wearer to lose hair on the area of the scalp where the hairs have been braided too tight. Please see page 40.
2. This is false. Please see page 40.
3. The answer to this question is "C," maybe, because the answer depends on the individual. Please see page 40.
4. "A," true, is the correct answer. Please see page 40.
5. The answer to this question is (drumroll) "B," false. Please see the first paragraph on page 39.

African Braiding Illustrated

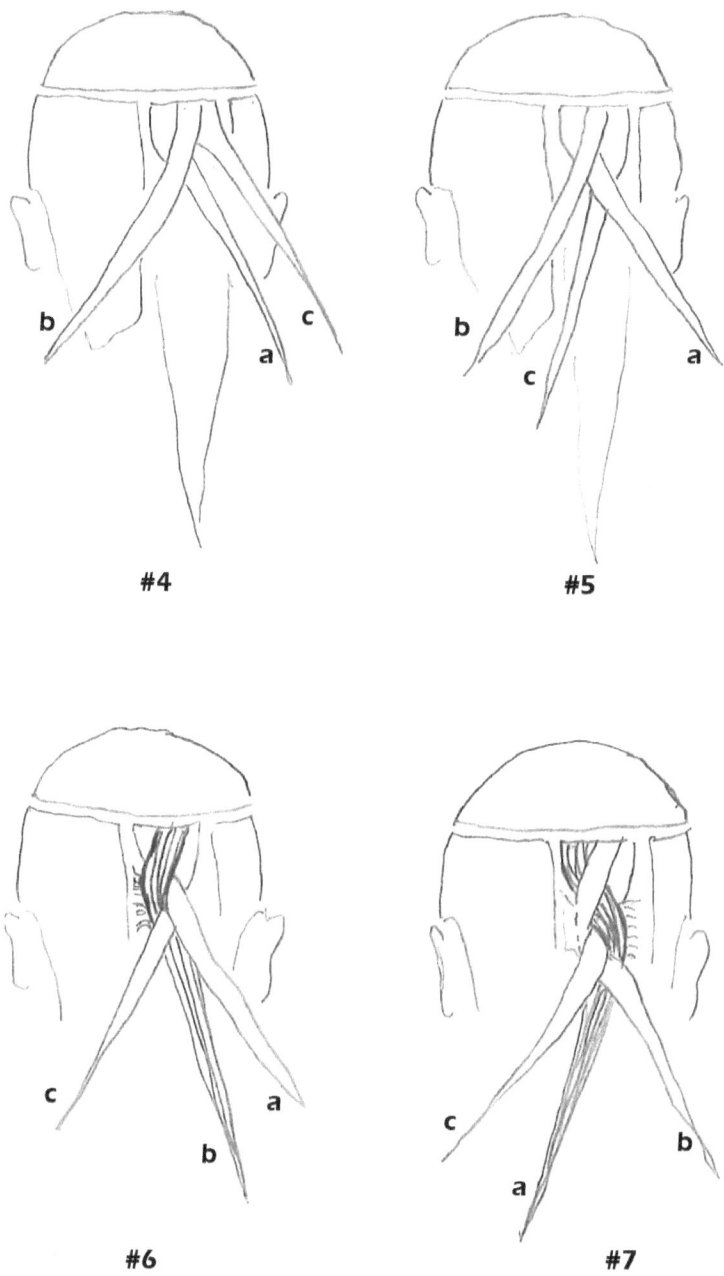

Repeat from here the motions of #6 and #7 to the bottom of the slice and then simply plait the hair to the ends of the fiber.

African Braiding Instructions

1. Section off a slice of hair to work with, as you did in the introductory paragraphs of this chapter.
2. At the top of the slice, horizontally separate a small amount of the hair *(strip)* from the rest of the slice.
3. Divide this strip into three equal parts *(strands)*.
4. Starting with the left strand, **pull it under** the center strand. This strand is now the center strand. What was the center strand is now the left strand.
5. Take the right strand, and pull it **under** the center strand. This strand is now the center strand. What was the center strand is now the right strand.
6. Take the left strand, and pull it **under** the center strand; include hair from the side as you pull this strand under the center strand. If the slice is very narrow, include hair from beneath. This strand is now the center strand. What was the center strand is now the left strand. Note that the hair included from the side or from beneath should be no larger than the width of the strand.
7. Take the right strand, and pull it **under** the center strand; include hair from the side/beneath as you pull this strand under the center strand. This strand is now the center strand. What was the center strand is now the right strand.
8. Repeat steps 6 and 7 to the bottom of the slice, and then simply plait the hair to the ends.

When African braiding, what you are doing is plaiting (see the section titled "Underhand Plaiting") the hair down to the scalp by including hair from the side/beneath of a slice as you plait the hair. **HOMEWORK #1:** Surprise!? Practice African braiding until you feel comfortable with this hairstyling method.

Following are sections concerning how to prepare and use fiber in the hair. Please read these sections before moving on to read the methods that I have developed for extending African braids. With this knowledge, you will be in a better position to minimize breakage on your real hair as you experiment with the methods for extending braids.

Preparing the Cut Bulk

In "Step One: The Preparation," you prepared the fiber for braiding, but there are other steps that you may wish to do before beginning any of the methods to extend braids. You may find that the following steps expedite the process of braiding extensions into your hair.

After washing and drying the fiber as described in "Step One: The Preparation," cut one-third of the fiber *(cut bulk)* away from the upper binding. **NOTE:** If you prefer very long braids, carefully cut and remove the rubber band binding of the bound end and separate one-third of the fiber from the rest of the fiber. We will still call this cut bulk. Lay the remaining two-thirds over to the side, out of your way.

Δ Be aware also, and remember, that fiber has weight. A long, thick piece of fiber on a small slice of hair may cause more breakage of the hair than a lesser width of fiber might.

Δ The cut bulk now may be either divided into widths no wider than one strand of the slice of hair to be braided (for a natural looking braid), or it may be separated as you braid your hair.

If you decide to divide the cut bulk before braiding, simply lay the strands over the back of a chair or other object (like an indoor clothes drying rack) to keep them within easy reach while braiding.

Δ Fiber Has Weight

The first time I cut my hair down to the scalp, it was an accident. After the initial shock, I got used to having very short hair, but after a while, and several intentional scalp cuts later, I decided to regrow my hair. Once it reached a length that was awkward to work with (too short to do anything with, too long to cut again), I decided to plait extensions into my hair. I had always wanted to put plaits in my hair that were almost long enough to sit on, and so that's what I did one day.

I left work one Friday with hair about four inches long that looked about one inch long (I was wearing my hair in an Afro) and returned the following Monday with plaits almost long enough to sit on. Most people at work thought that my hair looked nice, and just about everyone asked if it was my real hair. With a wide smile on my face, I told them yes, and that it had grown long overnight. After a few more inquiries, and stares of wonder, I 'fessed up, laughing as I admitted that I was wearing extensions in my hair. What a compliment! I had put the extensions in so well that most people thought that the plaits were my real hair. Even the people who said that they knew it wasn't my real hair kept looking at my hair as if to make sure that they were right.

This was my first time putting such long extensions in my hair. I had previously worn my hair in braids for one and a half years, but had only extended them as far as the middle of my back.

I left the long plaits in for about one week. They looked nice, but I didn't want to take the time to rebraid such long plaits.

I just wanted to share that story with you before you proceed to learn how to add extensions to your hair because it is important to understand that fiber has weight, and too much of it may break your hair off. I was able to plait my hair with such long extensions because I was very familiar with my hair. After years of working with my hair, I knew how much fiber I could add to my hair, and how large I would have to make the parts in my hair in order for it to accommodate the weight of the fiber, without the fiber breaking my hair off.

If this will be your first time working with extensions, follow the instructions above for separating the fiber in preparation for braiding—into widths no wider than one strand of the slice of hair to be braided. As you get to know your hair, and as you practice braiding with fiber, you will learn just how much, or how little, fiber you need to add to your hair in order for it to appear as if the fiber were part of your hair and not break your hair off.

Extending African Braids

Once again, as you did at the beginning of this chapter, section off a slice of hair to be extension braided. At the top of the slice, separate the strip from the rest of the hair. You are now ready to extend African braids by one of the following methods that you will learn in this book. I call these methods "Under and Around," "Under and Go", and "As You Go."

46 | *Hair Braiding to Grow, Strengthen, and Lengthen Your Hair*

Under and Around Illustrated

#1

fiber

#2

#3

#4

#5

Repeat from here the motions of #4 and #5 to the bottom of the slice and then simply plait the hair to the ends of the fiber. Note that "b" becomes the middle strand when you start to repeat #4, "c" becomes the left strand—give the hair part of "b" a tug to tighten and smooth down the braid.

Chapter 3 | Step Two: Methods of Braiding and Extending Your Hair | 47

Under and Around Instructions

1. Holding the strip <u>at the scalp near the roots</u> *(base)* and the fiber at its middle, place the fiber between the strip and the rest of the hair of the slice.
2. Wrap the strip over and around the middle of the fiber. If you are right-handed, the free ends of the strip should be to the right of the base. If you are left-handed, the free ends of the strip should be to the left of the base.
3. If you are right-handed, pull the strip over to the left and combine it with one-half of the fiber on that side. Left to right, you now have three strands: fiber, fiber/hair, fiber. If you are left-handed, pull the strip over to the right and combine it with one-half of the fiber on that side. Left to right, you now have three strands: fiber, hair/fiber, fiber. These strands are uneven. As you braid, even them out by taking a little from too-full strands and giving to strands that are not so full.
4. Starting with the left strand, pull it under the center strand; include hair from the side/beneath as you pull this strand under the center strand. This strand is now the center strand. What was the center strand is now the left strand.
5. Take the right strand, and pull it under the center strand; include hair from the side/beneath as you pull this strand under the center strand. This strand is now the center strand. What was the center strand is now the right strand.
6. Repeat steps 4 and 5 to the bottom of the slice and then simply plait the hair to the ends of the fiber.

Δ When you begin to braid the original center strand of step 3 (you will be repeating step 4 for the first time), it is a good idea to give the hair part of the fiber/hair (hair/fiber) combination a tug. This will tighten and smooth down the braid, helping to give the illusion that all the hairs (real and fiber) grow from your scalp.

This is the method (along with wrapping my hair up nightly with a scarf) that I used to braid my hair for one and a half years. This method allowed me to gently and securely braid in the small "baby" hairs along my hairline, which ended up growing out as long as the rest of my hair.

Under and Go Illustrated

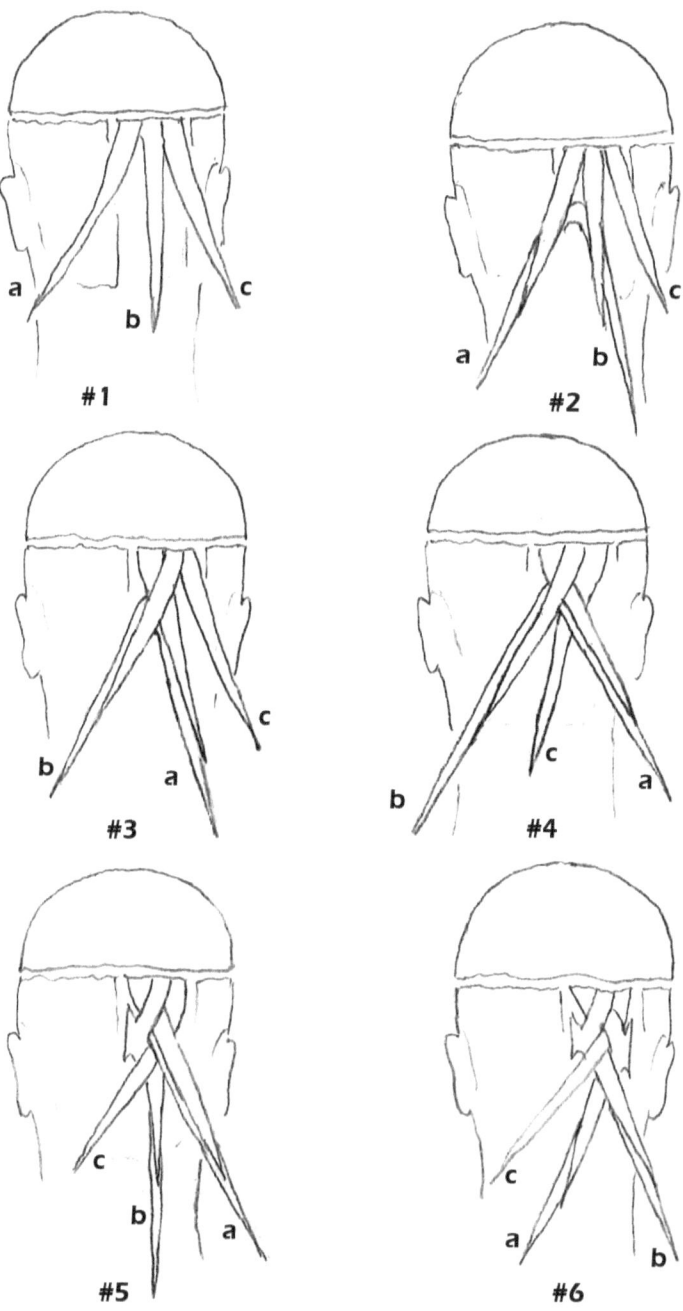

Repeat from here the motions of #5 and #6 to the bottom of the slice and then simply plait the hair to the ends of the fiber.

Under and Go Instructions

1. Divide the strip into three strands. If you are right-handed, the right strand should be slightly fuller than the other two strands. If you are left-handed, the left strand should be slightly fuller than the other two strands. A variation you may wish to try would be to divide the strip into three equal strands.
2. If you are right-handed, hold the fiber at its middle and place it beneath the left and center strands. You still have three strands: hair/fiber, hair/fiber, hair. If you are left-handed, place the fiber beneath the center and right strands. You still have three strands: hair, fiber/hair, fiber/hair. If you are doing the variation, place the fiber beneath the left and right strands. You still have three strands: hair/fiber, hair, fiber/hair.
3. To do this step correctly, whether you are doing the variation or not, allow the fiber to move as it will, but keep the fiber and hair combinations together. Starting with the left strand, pull it under the center strand. This strand is now the center strand. What was the center strand is now the left strand.
4. Take the right strand, and pull it under the center strand. This strand is now the center strand. What was the center strand is now the right strand.
5. Take the left strand, and pull it under the center strand; include hair from the side/beneath as you pull this strand under the center strand. This strand is now the center strand. What was the center strand is now the left strand.
6. Take the right strand, and pull it under the center strand; include hair from the side/beneath as you pull this strand under the center strand. This strand is now the center strand. What was the center strand is now the right strand.
7. Repeat steps 5 and 6 to the bottom of the slice, and then simply plait the hair to the ends of the fiber.

As You Go Illustrated

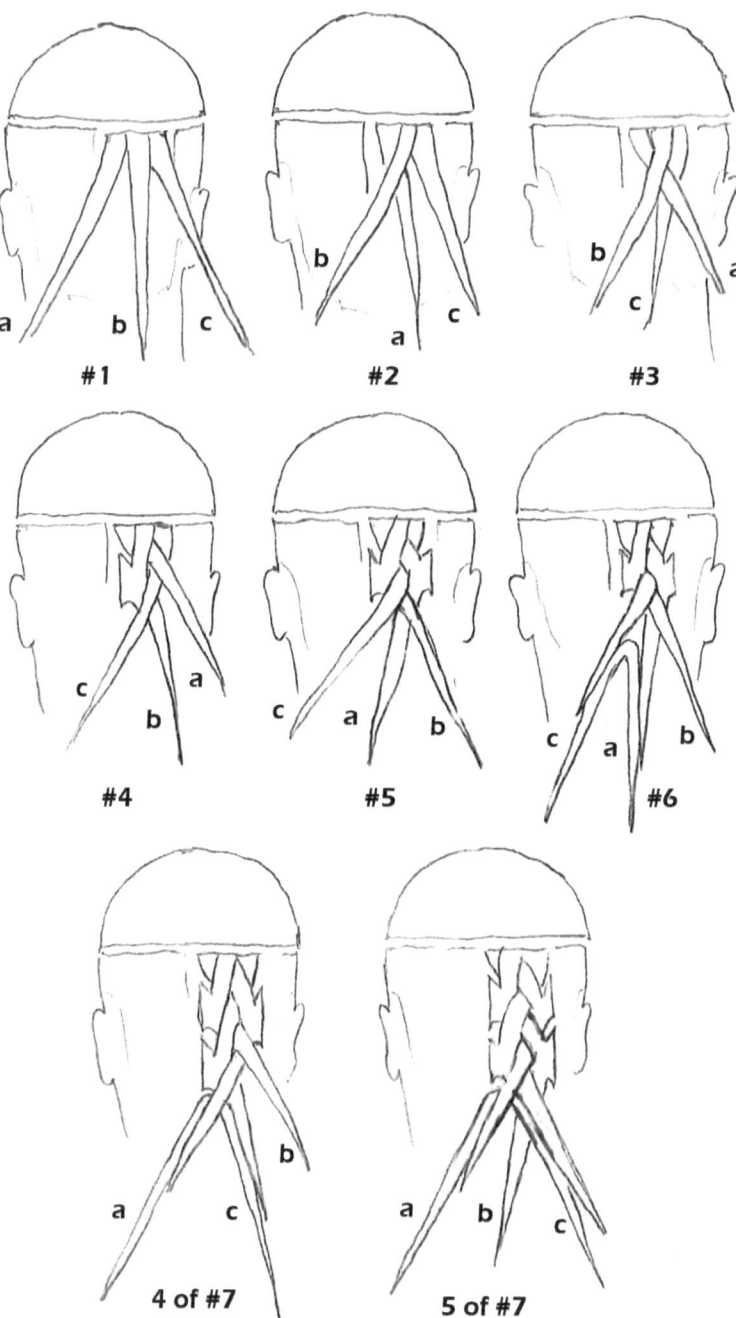

Repeat from here the motions of #4 and #5 to the bottom of the slice and then simply plait the hair to the ends of the fiber.

As You Go Instructions

1. Divide the strip into three equal strands.
2. Starting with the left strand, pull it under the center strand. This strand is now the center strand. What was the center strand is now the left strand.
3. Take the right strand, and pull it under the center strand. This strand is now the center strand. What was the center strand is now the right strand.
4. Take the left strand, and pull it under the center strand; include hair from the side/beneath as you pull this strand under the center strand. This strand is now the center strand. What was the center strand is now the left strand.
5. Take the right strand, and pull it under the center strand; include hair from the side/beneath as you pull this strand under the center strand. This strand is now the center strand. What was the center strand is now the right strand. Note that steps 4 and 5 are repeated not more than one-fourth of the length of the slice. When this point is reached, go on to step 6.
6. At this point, the extension is added. You should be just about to repeat step 4 (right-handed people), or step 5 (left-handed people). If you are right-handed, take the fiber to be added, and holding it at its middle, place it beneath the center and left strands. You still have three strands: hair/fiber, hair/fiber, hair. If you are left-handed, place the fiber to be added beneath the center and right strands. You still have three strands: hair, fiber/hair, fiber/hair.
7. To do this step correctly, allow the fiber to move as it will. Repeat steps 4 and 5 to the bottom of the slice, and then simply plait the hair to the ends of the fiber.

African Braiding Versus French Braiding

The difference between African and French braiding is that with French braiding the braid is inverted, because the left and right strands are pulled over the center strand as you include hair from the sides of a slice, as opposed to African braiding, where the left and right strands are pulled under the center strand as you include hair from the side/beneath of a slice.

French Braiding Illustrated

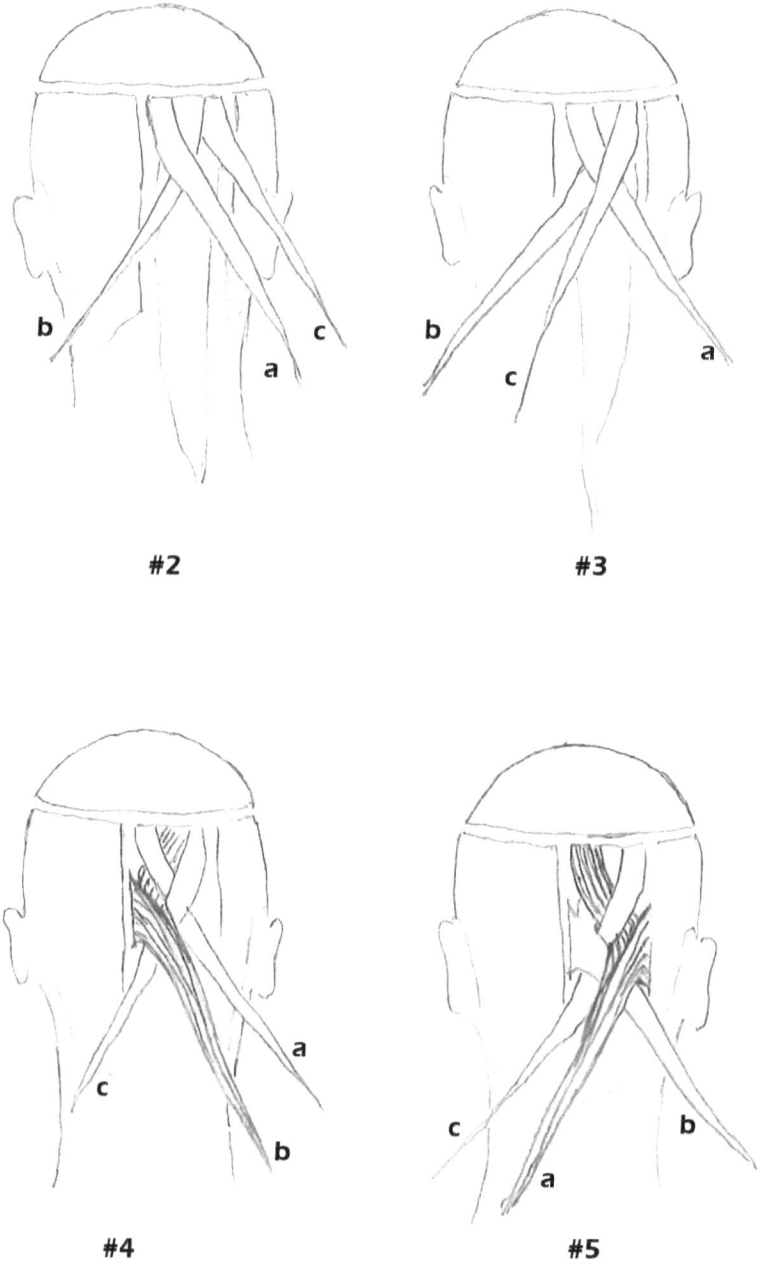

Repeat from here the motions of #4 and #5 to the bottom of the slice and then simply plait the hair to the ends of the fiber.

French Braiding Instructions

To me, French braids are more aesthetically pleasing when done in large sections. To practice the instructions below, part your hair as illustrated on the page to the left. You are now ready to French braid your hair.

1. Divide the strip into three equal strands.
2. Starting with the left strand, **pull it over** the center strand. This strand is now the center strand. What was the center strand is now the left strand.
3. Take the right strand, and pull it **over** the center strand. This strand is now the center strand. What was the center strand is now the right strand.
4. Take the left strand, and pull it **over** the center strand; include hair from the side as you pull this strand over the center strand. This strand is now the center strand. What was the center strand is now the left strand.
5. Take the right strand, and pull it **over** the center strand; include hair from the side as you pull this strand over the center strand. This strand is now the center strand. What was the center strand is now the right strand.
6. Repeat steps 4 and 5 to the bottom of the slice, and then simply plait the hair to the ends.

When French braiding, what you are doing is plaiting (see the section titled "Overhand Plaiting") the hair down to the scalp and including hair from the sides of a slice as you plait the hair. **HOMEWORK #2:** Practice French braiding until you feel comfortable with this hairstyling method.

Extending French Braids

As you did in the "French Braiding" instructions above, section off the first slice of hair to be extension braided. You also may wish to prepare the cut bulk as described in the section titled "Preparing the Cut Bulk." You are now ready to extend French braids by one of the following methods that you will learn in this book. I call these methods "Under and Go," and "As You Go."

Under and Go Illustrated

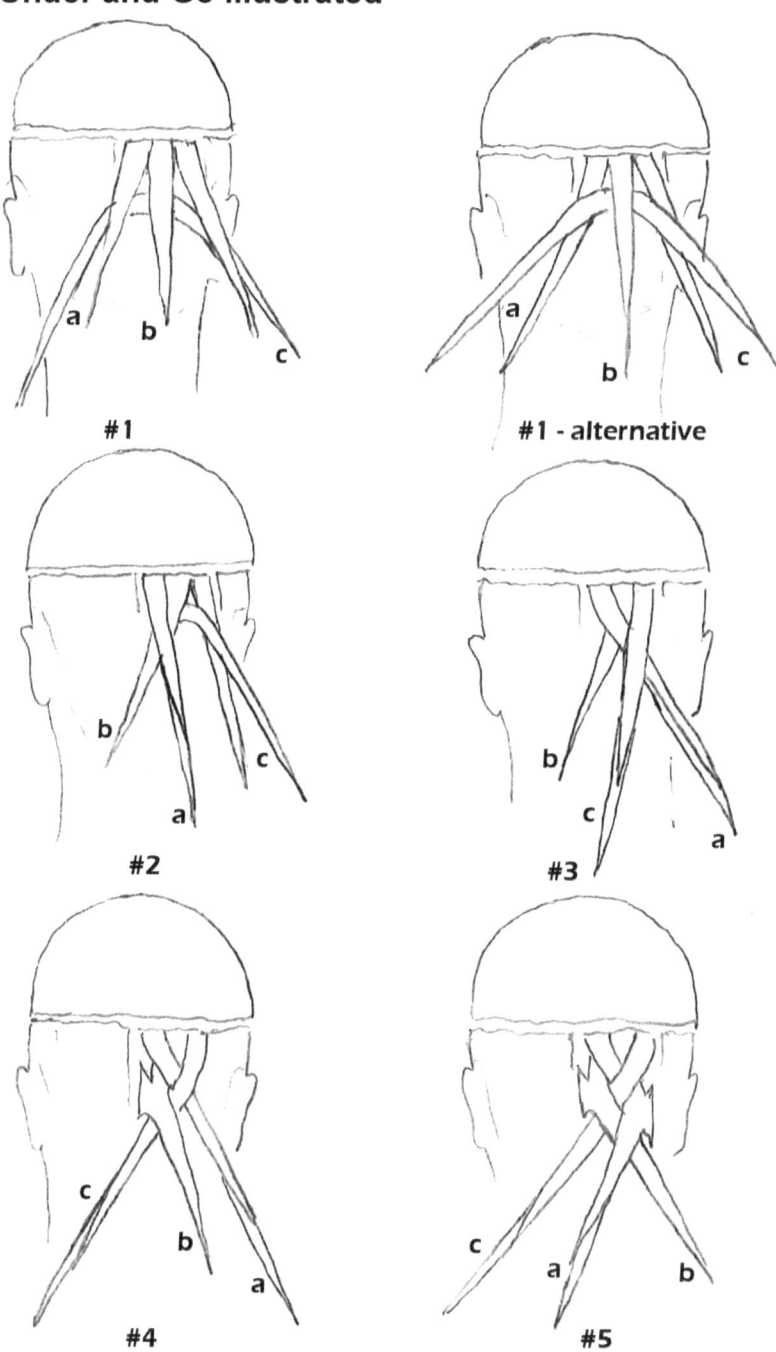

Repeat from here the motions of #4 and #5 to the bottom of the slice and then simply plait the hair to the ends of the fiber.

Under and Go Instructions

1. Holding the strip at the base, place the fiber between the strip and the rest of the hair of the slice. Combine the fiber with approximately one-fourth of the hair on either side of the strip. Your strands will be as follows: hair/fiber, hair, fiber/hair. Note that, as an alternative, the fiber may lie over the left strand, under the center strand, and over the right strand.
2. Starting with the left strand, pull it over the center strand. This strand is now the center strand. What was the center strand is now the left strand.
3. Take the right strand, and pull it over the center strand. This strand is now the center strand. What was the center strand is now the right strand.
4. Take the left strand, and pull it over the center strand; include hair from the side as you pull this strand over the center strand. This strand is now the center strand. What was the center strand is now the left strand.
5. Take the right strand, and pull it over the center strand; include hair from the side as you pull this strand over the center strand. This strand is now the center strand. What was the center strand is now the right strand.
6. Repeat steps 4 and 5 to the bottom of the slice, and then simply plait the hair to the ends of the fiber.

As You Go Illustrated

#1

#2

#3

#4

#5

#6

4 of #7

5 of #7

Repeat from here the motions of #4 and #5 to the bottom of the slice and then simply plait the hair to the ends of the fiber.

As You Go Instructions

1. Divide the strip into three equal strands.
2. Starting with the left strand, pull it over the center strand. This strand is now the center strand. What was the center strand is now the left strand.
3. Take the right strand, and pull it over the center strand. This strand is now the center strand. What was the center strand is now the right strand.
4. Take the left strand, and pull it over the center strand; include hair from the side as you pull this strand over the center strand. This strand is now the center strand. What was the center strand is now the left strand.
5. Take the right strand, and pull it over the center strand; include hair from the side as you pull this strand over the center strand. This strand is now the center strand. What was the center strand is now the right strand. Note that steps 4 and 5 are repeated not more than one-fourth of the length of the slice. When this point is reached, go on to step 6.
6. At this point, the extension is added. Take the fiber to be added, and, holding it at its middle, place it beneath the left and right strands. You still have three strands: hair/fiber, hair, fiber/hair.
7. Repeat steps 4 and 5 to the bottom of the slice, and then simply plait the hair to the ends of the fiber.

The process of adding extensions to African braids, and French braids, is difficult at best. However, the more you practice the better you will become.

Plaiting Your Hair

Plaiting is the basis of all braided styles. Let's begin by squaring off a large section of hair to work with at the back of your head. Reach your hands to the back of your head and separate that hair into three even strands. You are now ready to plait your hair by one of the following methods that you will learn in this book. These methods are known as underhand plaiting and overhand plaiting.

58 | *Hair Braiding to Grow, Strengthen, and Lengthen Your Hair*

Underhand Plaiting Illustrated

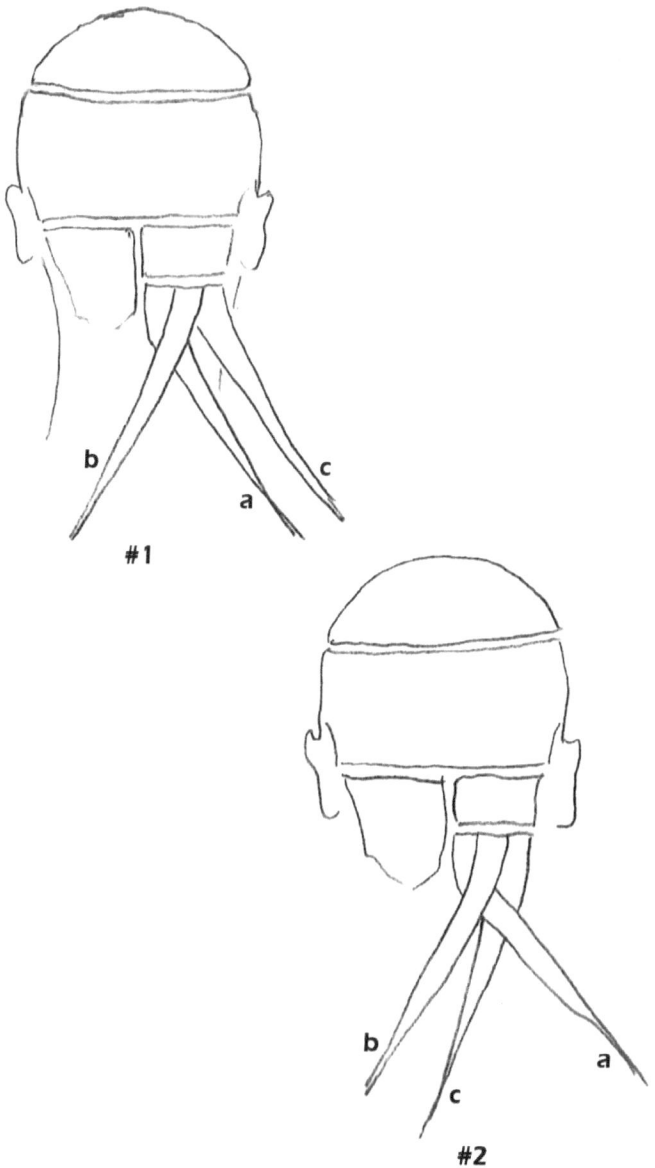

Repeat from here the motions of #1 and #2 to the ends of your hair.

Underhand Plaiting Instructions

1. Take the hair that you separated out according to the instructions in "Plaiting Your Hair" at the bottom of page 57, and starting with the left strand, pull it under the center strand. This strand is now the center strand. What was the center strand is now the left strand.
2. Take the right strand and pull it under the center strand. This strand is now the center strand. What was the center strand is now the right strand.
3. Repeat steps 1 and 2 to the ends of your hair. **NOTE:** This method of plaiting the hair is used in all African braided hairstyles.

Take Note

The term "underhand plaiting" comes from the fact that you are pulling the strands "under the hand" as you repeat the motions to plait the hair. Likewise, the term "overhand plaiting" comes from the fact that you are pulling the strands "over the hand" as you plait the hair.

Overhand Plaiting Illustrated

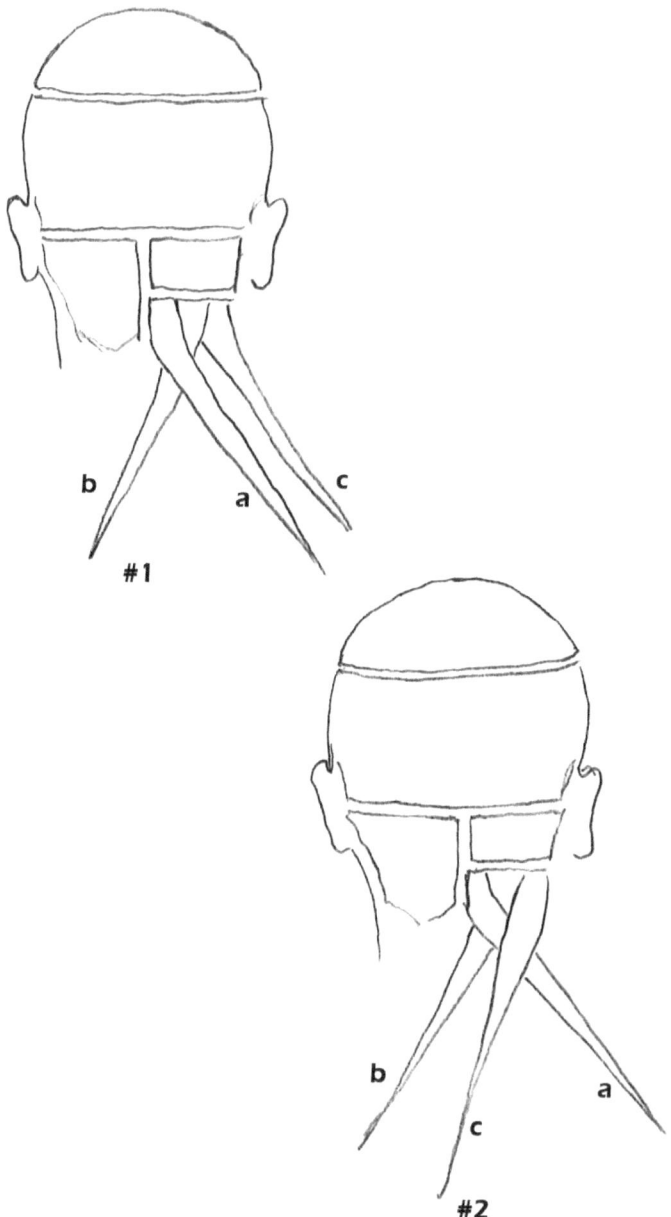

Repeat from here the motions of #1 and #2 to the ends of your hair.

Overhand Plaiting Instructions

1. Take the hair that you separated out according to the instructions in "Plaiting Your Hair" at the bottom of page 57, and starting with the left strand, pull it over the center strand. This strand is now the center strand. What was the center strand is now the left strand.
2. Take the right strand and pull it over the center strand. This strand is now the center strand. What was the center strand is now the right strand.
3. Repeat steps 1 and 2 to the ends of your hair. **NOTE:** This method of plaiting the hair is used in all French braided hairstyles.

Extending Plaits

I believe that extended plaits are an artistic hairstyle, not a wig. I've seen some plaited styles where the plaits have not been plaited to the ends of the fiber and are so small that it almost looks as though the wearer is actually wearing a wig of loose hair. This can't be good for the hair.

Δ Try to limit the width of your plaits so that you can easily rebraid your hair, and so that the fiber won't break it off during the removal process. I believe that one-half inch is the smallest amount of hair that you should try to plait, but that is really up to you and what you are trying to accomplish—a temporary hairstyle, or hair growth. Never leave most of the length of your hair extensions (especially the hair/fiber combinations) in an unplaited state. Always plait to the ends of the fiber to avoid hair loss from breakage and split ends. If you really want to plait your hair in plaits smaller than one-half inch, and leave some of it in an unplaited state, see a licensed professional. Treat this type of hairstyle as a temporary hairstyle for a special occasion. Once the occasion is over, return to that same hairstylist to have the plaits properly removed.

Now, before we begin extending plaits, prepare the fiber as described in the section titled "Preparing the Cut Bulk." At the back of your head, section off about a square inch of hair to work with for this next exercise. You are now ready to plait extensions into your hair by one of the following methods that you will learn in this book. I call these methods "Underplait," "Overplait," and "Preplait."

Underplait Illustrated

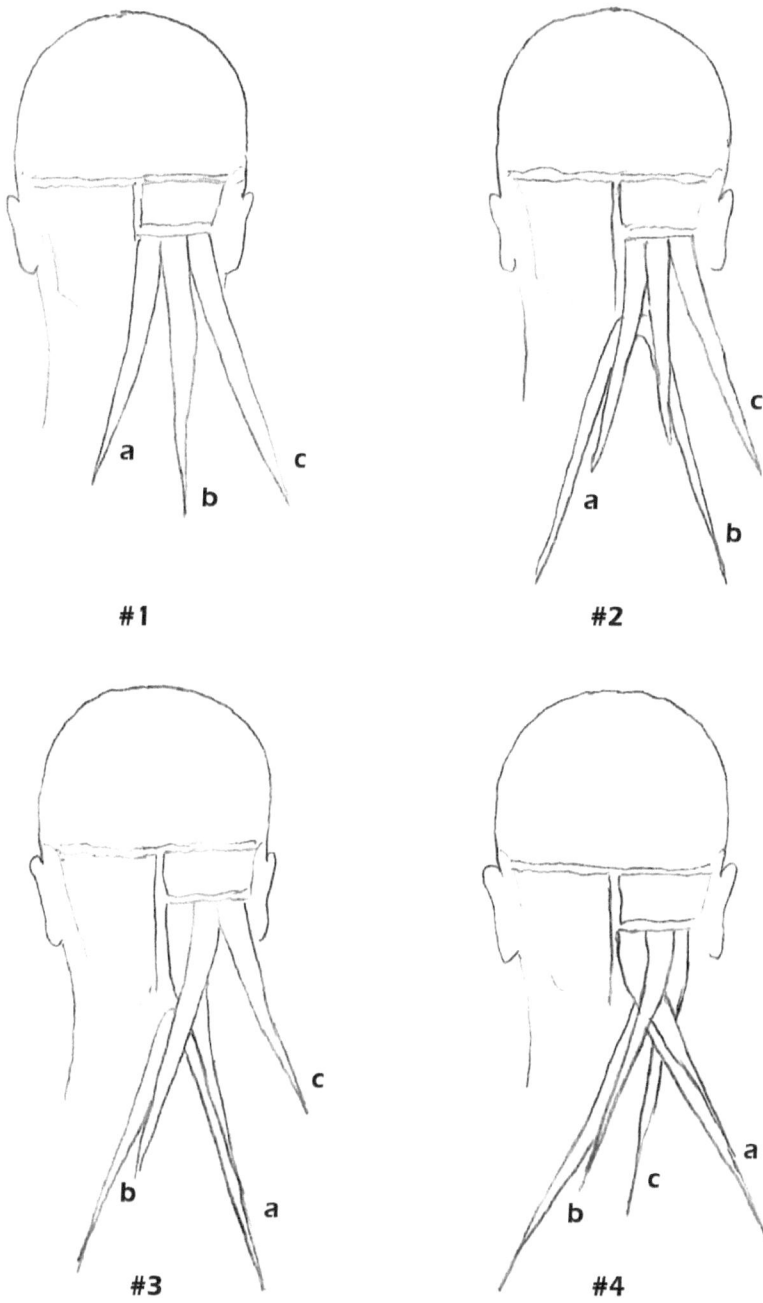

Repeat from here the motions of #3 and #4 to the ends of the fiber.

Underplait Instructions

1. Divide the section of hair to be extended into three strands. If you are right-handed, the right strand should be slightly fuller than the other two strands. If you are left-handed, the left strand should be slightly fuller than the other two strands.
2. If you are right-handed, take the fiber to be added, and holding it at its middle, place it beneath the center and left strands. You still have three strands: hair/fiber, hair/fiber, hair. If you are left-handed, place the fiber to be added beneath the center and right strands. You still have three strands: hair, fiber/hair, fiber/hair.
3. Starting with the left strand (allow the fiber to move as it will, but keep the hair and fiber combinations together), pull it under the center strand. This strand is now the center strand. What was the center strand is now the left strand.
4. Take the right strand, and pull it under the center strand. This strand is now the center strand. What was the center strand is now the right strand.
5. Repeat steps 3 and 4 to the ends of the fiber.

64 | *Hair Braiding to Grow, Strengthen, and Lengthen Your Hair*

Overplait Illustrated

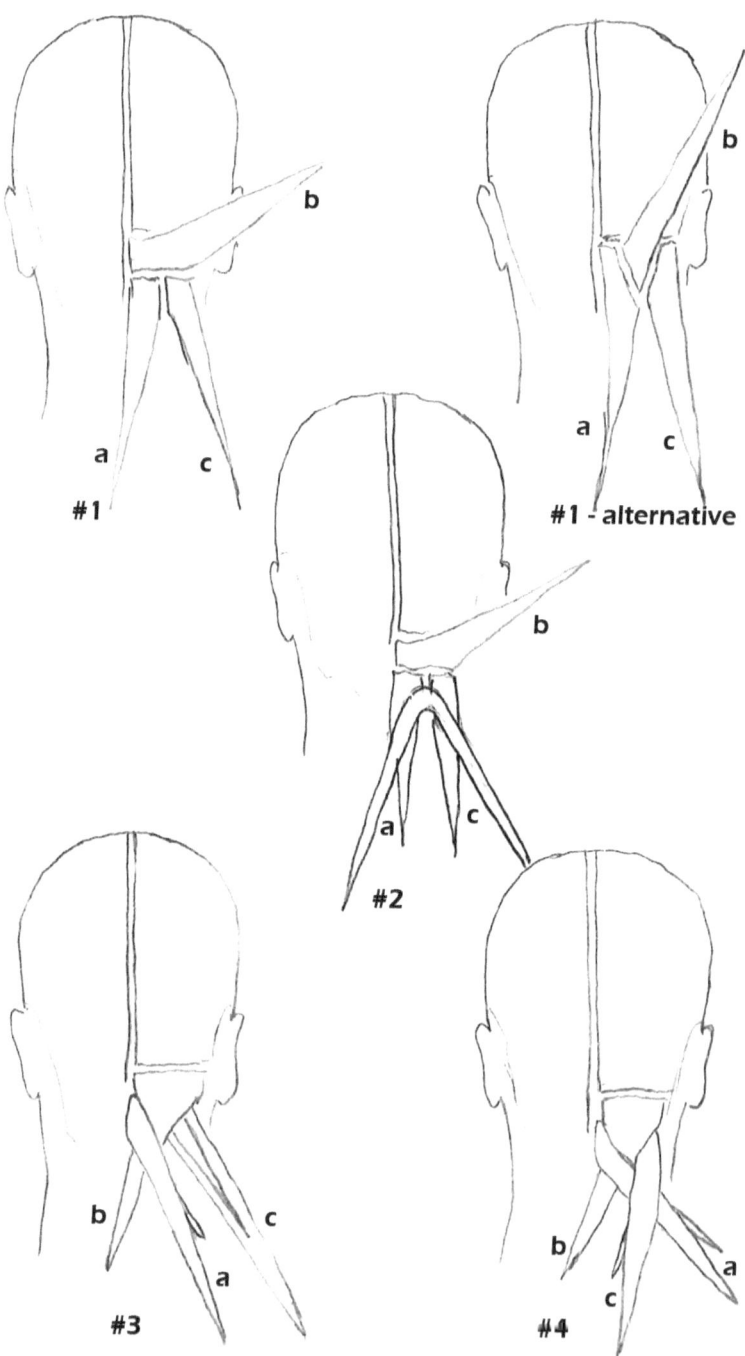

Repeat from here the motions of #3 and #4 to the ends of the fiber.

Overplait Instructions

1. Using your fingers, horizontally divide the section to be extended in half. Next, vertically divide the lower section in half. An alternative placement method that you may wish to try would be to diagonally divide the section to be extended into three triangular sections: part the hair diagonally from the upper corners (start one-fourth the width of the section from the outer edges) down to slightly over the center so that the two diagonals appear to overlap.
2. Take the fiber to be added, and holding it at its middle, place it over the two strands of the lower section you just divided in step 1, above. If you are doing the alternative, place the fiber over the left strand, under the center strand, and over the right strand.
3. Starting with the left strand, pull it over the center strand. This strand is now the center strand. What was the center strand is now the left strand.
4. Take the right strand, and pull it over the center strand. This strand is now the center strand. What was the center strand is now the right strand.
5. Repeat steps 3 and 4 to the ends of the fiber.

Preplait Illustrated

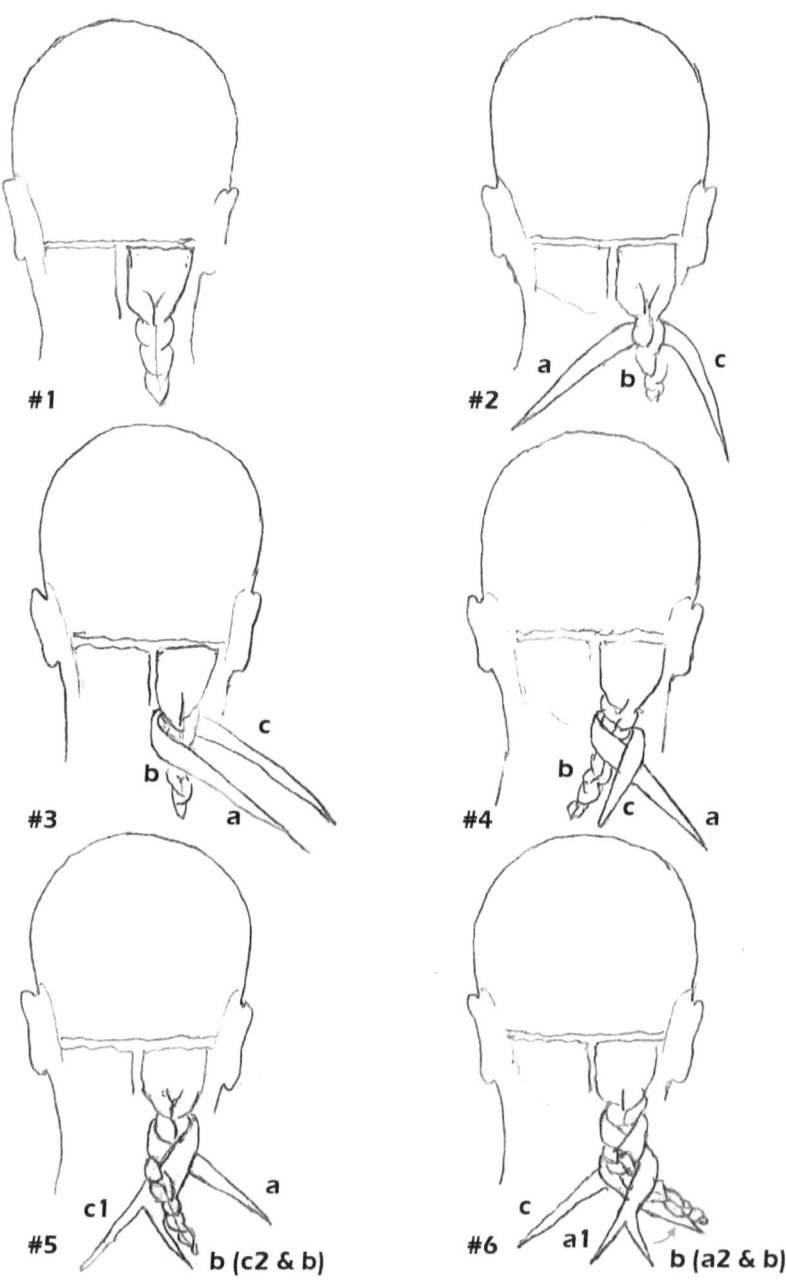

NOTE: If your hair is very short, an alternative to try instead of #2 above would be to wrap the plaited hair around the fiber as is done with the "Under and Around" method of extending African braids, skip #3 and #4 and proceed to #5 and #6, repeat from there the motions of #3 and #4 to the ends of the fiber.

Preplait Instructions

1. Overhand plait the section to be extended.
2. Take the fiber to be added, and holding it at its middle, place it beneath the hair that you just plaited, at the base. You will have three strands: fiber, the hair you just plaited, and fiber. **NOTE:** If your hair is very short, an alternative to try would be to wrap the plaited hair around the fiber as is done with the "Under and Around" method of extending African braids, and proceed to step 5 at "***combine***."
3. Starting with the left strand, pull it over the center strand. This strand is now the center strand. What was the center strand is now the left strand.
4. Take the right strand, and pull it over the center strand. This strand is now the center strand. What was the center strand is now the right strand.
5. At this point, tricky hand motion is necessary. Repeat step 3, **BUT**, after you have pulled the left strand over the center strand, **combine** what is now the center strand (the plaited hair) with some of the fiber from what is now the left strand. For the alternative, go to step 6 at "***pull***."
6. Again, tricky hand motion is needed for this step. Repeat step 4, **BUT**, after you have ***pull***ed the right strand over the center strand, combine what is now the right strand with some of the fiber from what is now the center strand.
7. Repeat steps 3 and 4 to the ends of the fiber. **NOTE:** This method of extending plaits is the most difficult to do, and the hardest to maintain. It is useful for extending plaits that are two inches or less in length. It is important that the person using this extension method not pull or tug the hair as the extensions may slip out. Be aware that even if you do not pull or tug your hair during washing, the extensions may still slip out if your hair is very short because the water, shampoo, and conditioner help to loosen the extensions. Steps 5 and 6 are "must-dos" because these steps help "anchor" the fiber to the plait, which helps to keep the extension from slipping out of the plait too soon after the style has been finished.

Take Note

Δ When using the Preplait method to extend plaits, frequently redoing some of the plaits (more than once a week) may be necessary to tighten the plaits in order to avoid extensions slipping out. Also, it is necessary to maintain the real hair by replaiting it at least every two weeks (weekly if you are braiding permed hair) to avoid buildup in the real hair. **NOTE:** If you do not replait the real hair when redoing the Preplait method, your real hair may *loc*. I originally used my Preplait method on permed hair that I wanted to grow out. I did not redo my real hair weekly. My hair *matted* so bad from buildup that I had to cut the plaits out.

Also note that, because the width of the strands start out uneven when you are extending plaits, you must remember to even them out when beginning step 5, for example, in each of the methods of extending plaits. This helps to give the plaits a more realistic appearance.

Some Things to Think About

In this chapter you have learned how to African braid, French braid, and plait hair. You also learned how to extend each of these styling methods in such a way that the fiber is not easily detectable.

With any method of braiding or extending, as someone once said, practice makes perfect. Therefore, practice and experiment with these styling methods to find the method that works best for you. For example, if you are right-handed, try the instructions for left-handed people. If you are left-handed, try the instructions for right-handed people to see if you get a better look. The Under and Go method of extending African braids offers a variety of possibilities. For example, if you are right-handed, try placing the fiber beneath the center and right strands (as left-handed persons are instructed to do). Note that the left strand would be slightly fuller than the center and right strands. Next, you would start braiding with the left strand as step 3 instructs.

If you are using fiber to extend your braided style, after you have braided all sections the ends may seem uneven. You may want to trim them so that the braids appear neat and somewhat even, but not to the point where they would easily unravel. Now that you know how to braid, you are ready for "Step Three. Braid Care."

Chapter 4
| *Step Three: Braid Care*

In "Step Two: Methods of Braiding and Extending Your Hair" you learned to African braid, French braid, plait, and how to extend these styling methods with fiber. In "Step Three: Braid Care" you will learn how to care for these styling methods.

In chapter 1, "Understanding My African Hair" I listed some of the reasons women and men of today enjoy wearing creative and simplistic braided styles: cultural; as a way to grow hair longer; as a resting phase for damaged hair; as a beautification or aesthetic grooming tool, like makeup, earrings, or fingernail polish; as a practical answer to aid a demanding business schedule; and obviously, simply because the wearer chooses to style her/his hair in braided styles.

I mention this now because you should again consider your own reasons for wearing braids/extensions. Your answer(s) will determine how you care for your chosen style. You owe it to yourself to take responsibility for caring for your own hair by noticing how you are treating it yourself and how it responds to different hair care products and styles.

Several factors will be discussed in this chapter that will affect the growth of your hair while you are wearing braids—with or without extensions. These include: Hair Ornaments and Styling—including the use of rubber bands, Daily Care, Weekly Care, Rebraiding, Brushing Your Hair Again, the Afro, and Working with Hairstylists.

Hair Ornaments and Styling

From day to day you may wish to change the appearance of your braids by utilizing the aid of various hair styling ornaments: bobby pins, hair bows, decorative combs, curls, etc.

Δ These styling aids may help to add versatility to what otherwise could be a very monotonous hairstyle; however, they also may cause damage to the hair. To avoid this as much as possible, you should avoid using any ornament that: will snag your hair, is not easily removable for sleep, is painful, is uncomfortable, or puts too much weight on your hair. A good example of the above would be a bobby pin where the rounded tip is coming off or missing because a bobby pin in this state could snag the hair, causing split ends.

As mentioned above, sometimes you may wish to curl your braids. When wearing extensions, it is usually best to curl the braids with cold curlers as soon as you have finished a new style or just after rebraiding. If you wish to use hot curlers, it is best if you curl only the part of the braid that is all fiber.

Δ **Use Rubber Bands Safely with the *CURB System***

Ordinarily, I would not endorse using rubber bands on your hair, but my sister has discovered an ingenious, novel, and safe way to use them on your hair that may help minimize breakage. I refer to this system as the *CURB* ("*Correctly Using Rubber Bands*") *System*.

If you are in the process of braiding your hair, try to use scrunchies. If you use rubber bands during the braiding process do not wrap them around the hair so tightly that it will be difficult to quickly remove them from your hair.

If you desire to use rubber bands in order to hold a finished style in place (for example, ponytails that consist of many braids), make sure that you apply your oil, grease, or leave-in conditioner to the rubber bands before you use them on your hair in order to help minimize breakage.

To remove rubber bands from your hair, or your child's hair, you will need the ball-tipped seam ripper with a safety cover listed in "Step Three" of the "Materials You Will Need" section of chapter 1, "Understanding My African Hair." My sister loves to use rubber bands on her daughter's hair to hold her loose hairs—and her braids when her hair is braided—neatly together in ponytails. She then wraps stylish bows or ribbons around the rubber bands on her daughter's hair. My niece may lose her hair bows, but at least her hair style remains in place because of the rubber bands. To safely remove the rubber bands, my sister uses a seam ripper as follows:

1. Hold the ponytail stationary in one of your hands at the point where the rubber band binding wraps around the hair.
2. Using your fingers, and the seam ripper, gently lift up one of the bands of the rubber band binding.
3. As you use the seam ripper to hold the band up and away from your hair and scalp, hold onto the rest of the rubber band binding on the ponytail (so that the rubber band does not tighten into, and strangle the hair), and push the seam ripper up and away from your head, or your child's head, until the band breaks.
4. Gently unwrap the rubber band binding from around the ponytail.

Take Note
The CURB System is a great way to avoid hair loss that can be attributed to using rubber bands on your hair. Breakage can occur when you remove rubber bands by simply pulling the rubber band off the hair in one swift movement.

You can tell whether or not you have hair breakage from rubber band usage by wrapping one around a ponytail in your usual manner, and then using your hands to gently smooth the hair lying on your scalp away from the ponytail. If any hairs move away from the ponytail, note the length of the hair from the scalp to the point of the rubber band binding. If these hairs meet up at the point of the rubber band binding, you probably have hair breakage due to rubber band usage/removal, and should start using my sister's CURB System to minimize breakage, and safely use rubber bands on you and your children's hair.

Daily Care
As a part of your daily hair care routine, whenever you have free time during the day you may wish to try a scalp massage. Do this by placing your hands on either side of your head and then gently using your palms to move your scalp in circular motions toward your face. Use the pads of your fingers to do the same along your

hairline areas. If this is painful, your braids may be in too tight. Try rebraiding the area that is painful.

If you wear your hair in braids during the winter months, I recommend that you wear a cap with a satin lining, or use a satin scarf or stocking cap with a cap, whenever you go outside or are in a cold area indoors. The cap will help you to avoid a cold and the satin scarf/stocking cap will help to keep your braids neat. Also, whenever you sleep, it is a good idea to secure your braids with a satin scarf/stocking cap.

Using scarves will help to keep your braids looking neat from day to day, but you must be careful when you remove them from around your head. Whipping a scarf off of your head may "catch" some hairs in the fabric of the scarf, causing split ends to start, or worsen. In order to keep your braids as neat as possible, and avoid split ends, untie a scarf and gently slip it off of your head.

Although hair-care experts usually recommend using silk scarves, I've used cotton ones, too. Again, experiment to see if one type of scarf works better for you over another type.

Weekly Care

It is a good idea to wash and rebraid your hair at least once a week while wearing it braided. Weekly washing and rebraiding help to combat the possible buildup of dust, oil, sweat, dead skin cells, lint, and odor. Because these elements can combine to weaken and damage your hair, try not to go more than one week without washing your braids. Weekly braiding, with all that it entails, also forces you to get to know your hair better.

Eventually you will discover your own method of washing your braids; however, you may wish to use the following method until you do.

1. Do not unbraid your hair. To expedite the braiding process, you will wash your hair with the braids in. The best way to wash your hair—whether it is loose or braided—is to wash it in the shower or use a shower attachment in the bathtub. The objective is to not bunch your hair up, but to keep it in a straight-up-and-down position. **NOTE:** If you decided to put very long braids in your hair (see the "Fiber Has Weight," section in "Step Two: Methods of Braiding and Extending

Your Hair"), you may want to cut the length of the fiber before you wash your braids and use fresh fiber to rebraid your hair if you want to retain the length. If you can't remember where the hair/fiber combinations end, carefully unbraid one braid in the back of your head (or the braid that you know contains the longest length of your real hair) and stretch that hair out to its full length. Use it as a guide to cut the rest of the braids a little below that point. Rebraid that hair.
2. Begin washing your hair by thoroughly wetting it in the shower.
3. Pour your shampoo into the palms of your hands and work up a small lather.
4. Squeeze the shampoo through your braids, gently pressing it into your scalp.
5. Run your fingers up and down the parts, gently scratching in a side-to-side motion, to help remove buildup. As you do this gentle scratching motion, you are gently moving the braids as you scratch so that you also scratch beneath the braids.
6. Separate a group of braids and squeeze the lather down the length of them by intermittently opening and closing your fist down their length to the ends of the braids. Repeat, and then do the remaining sections. **NOTE:** Look at the color of the shampoo. If it isn't white (or whatever color the manufacturer says that it should be), repeat this step after you do step 7.
7. Rinse the shampoo from your hair using the same motions that you used to shampoo your hair.
8. If you use a wash-out conditioner, condition your hair and rinse the conditioner from your hair using the same motions that you used to shampoo your hair. If possible, it is best to allow your hair to dry naturally.

∆ Rebraiding

After washing and drying your hair, you will notice that your braids seem loose. This is due both to washing and new growth. Rebraiding will help to avoid *matting*, and friction on the new growth from the loose braids.

You may wish to rebraid the front sections first. The strategy here is that if you cannot complete all sections in one sitting, you can always pull all of the braids to the back of your head into one plait to cover up any unbraided sections, and re-do any remaining sections later. For now, select a section to work with, and secure all of the other sections out of your way. Rebraid each section one braid at a time, securing all of the other braids in the section out of your way as you work. To keep your braids neat looking, rebraid each section from left to right if you're right-handed; from right to left if you are left-handed.

Until you develop your own method of rebraiding, try using the following method to rebraid your hair one braid at a time.

1. Gently unplait the braid from the ends up to the base. Be especially careful when you reach your real hair. Never harshly pull, tug, or use any type of comb or brush while rebraiding. Patiently and gently work with the braid, using your fingers.

2. If you are reusing the fiber, once you have removed it from the strip, lay it over to the side for now. If you are not reusing the fiber that you just removed from your hair, you should have already prepared the new fiber for your hair according to the "Preparing the Fiber" instructions in "Step One: The Preparation."

3. Gently finger-comb your real hair. When you run into resistance, stop and gently work it out with your fingers. You will see what may appear to be a large amount of hair. This is hair that fell out due to hereditary conditions, your hair's growth cycle, or was broken by you during the braiding/unbraiding process. If you feel that the hair loss is excessive, consult your physician. **NOTE:** If there is buildup near the scalp, detangle that area first. To do this, for example, if you are detangling plaits, using the fingers of both hands, gently pull the hair (at the point of the buildup) out and away from the buildup. It is usually best to start at the edges of the buildup and work your way toward the middle using a side-to-side motion. Do not use an up/down motion to detangle the buildup. That type of motion may cause clumps of hair to break off. Note that with braids (as opposed to plaits) you may want to try squaring off sections of the slice at a time to detangle, particularly if a lot of buildup is present.

4. If you are using fresh fiber, skip this step. Finger-comb the fiber so that you can use it again. Holding it firmly and slightly off-center, use your thumb, index, and middle fingers as a comb, running them down the length of the fiber. When you run into resistance, stop and gently work it out with your fingers. When you finish finger-combing this side, do the other side. NOTE: The individual hairs of the fiber will be uneven. This is what you want as it aids in making the fiber appear natural after it has been rebraided back into your real hair.
5. At this point, if you wish, apply a small dab of grease to the hair of the slice and the fiber. I prefer using a leave-in conditioner.
6. You are now ready to rebraid this braid using one of the methods of "Step Two: Methods of Braiding and Extending Your Hair."
7. Repeat steps 1 through 6 for the next braid.

Take Note
Detangling the fiber and your real hair is important. It helps to avoid matting of your real hair.

△ Also, take special notice of your hairline. If it, or any other area on your scalp, appears more sparse than usual, you may be braiding your hair too tight, or the fiber may be too thick or long to be supported by the slice of hair into which it has been braided.

After you have rebraided all sections, the ends may seem uneven. You may want to trim them so that the braids appear neat and somewhat even, but not to the point where they would easily unravel.

△ If you have been carefully rebraiding your hair for at least three to four months, and you have not noticed any new growth near your scalp, you may want to consult a physician to see if there is any medical reason as to why your hair is not growing. My hair seems to grow anywhere from one-fourth inch to one-half inch a month. It also seems to grow slower during the winter months.

The Final Unbraiding
At one period in my life, I wore my hair braided in the same style,

using the same fiber, over and over again, for one and a half years. When the fiber became too short due to the growth of my hair to insert folded even two-thirds its length, rather than in the middle, I decided to unbraid my hair completely.

When taking your braids out completely, unbraid a section at a time, detangling each braid with your fingers. Halfway through the section that you're working on, plait the hairs together, and then continue and do the remaining sections the same way. The object is to have at least four large plaits by the time you finish unbraiding your hair. At this point in the process, do not comb or brush your hair.

Δ   Wash your hair with the plaits in and towel dry it. While your hair is still wet, unplait one plait and comb it from the ends up to the scalp. For this, I use a smooth Afro pick with no jagged edges. If you run into resistance, use your fingers to gently work it out. It also helps to wet the pick (not your hair) when you run into resistance, and then continue using it to comb your hair. Replait and do the remaining plaits. **NOTE:** My hair sits up and away from my scalp. An Afro pick can reach down through the depths of my hair so that I am combing all hairs in a section at one time. An Afro comb, on the other hand, would only allow me to comb the "top" hairs, leaving the hairs not visible still tangled.

If you keep your braids in for any length of time, as I did, be prepared for what will appear to be a lot of hair in your comb (pick). Remember that you are using a comb now as opposed to finger combing your hair, and you are combing more than one braid at a time. I will admit that I was in shock at the amount of hair that initially came out in my comb when It started to comb my hair again. Then I realized that the amount of hair that I was seeing was normal due to the reasons that I've just stated.

Also, you may have a painful scalp for a few days. I came to realize that this, like the amount of hair that I was combing out in my comb, was largely due to the fact that my hair had been growing in a confined state. Another thing to note is that, depending on your hair type and the width of your braids, your hair will probably seem to be more textured than usual.

To help your hair, and yourself, readjust to its loose-growing state, try wearing it in large French braids, or large plaits, for a week or more. During this time you may find it easier to wash your hair with the French braids or plaits in while you readjust to styling "loose" hair.

If you're going to wear your hair in a loose state for a while, consider training it to comb easier by smoothing your shampoo down the length of your hair after you've lathered up. Rinse using the same motions. When you apply wash-out conditioner, smooth it down the length of your hair, too. The idea is to smooth each of the products down the length of your hair until it feels like the tight curl of your hair is a looser and more uniform curl. I used to finger comb and smooth my hair like this for about five minutes each time I washed it. I'd actually forgotten about doing this, but someone recently said that if they had the choice of working on my hair, or someone else's hair that might have a tighter curl, they'd rather work on my hair. I can tell you that my curl is as tight as that of a lot of other African American women. It may *look* different because of the smoothing process I've just described, and have done for years, but it is the *same* tight curl.

One other thing that I would like to note here is that as I have gotten older, I have started to notice a dryness in my skin and hair. To alleviate and combat this dryness, I have taken to using a trick of one of my mother's sisters. She applies an oil to her skin nightly, and she looks like she's about thirty years younger than her real age. A twist on this that works for me is to pour warm coconut oil on my hair, place a plastic cap over my head, wrap a towel over that, and let it sit overnight. (Don't use the good sheets!) I wash the oil out in the morning, and the feel of my scalp and hair is remarkable. Of course, the oil makes its way down my face and neck while I sleep, so my face gets a good coating, too. (I would like to caution you here to wipe as much of the oil off of your face as you can before you go to sleep in order to prevent it from getting into your eyes as you sleep.) I try to oil my hair now at least once a month with coconut oil. I have tried avocado and olive oils as well. I prefer the coconut oil. I have since learned that some Indians (India) do this daily. They refer to this process as "oiling" the hair. It's like the African American concept of greasing the scalp, except they wash the oil from their hair either after letting it sit for a few minutes or the next day, while we do not. Based on how my aunt looks, I think that washing the oil from your skin and hair daily is better for you.

∆ Brushing Your Hair Again

Until your scalp feels "normal" again, it would probably be a good idea to not brush your hair. But when you feel it is okay to start brushing your hair again, keep in mind the texture of your hair, and the strength of your hand.

I have hair that is very tightly curled, so I use a hard boar-bristle brush that is reinforced with nylon bristles. After combing the tangles out of my hair and applying a leave-in conditioner, I'll brush it with my brush—just enough to smooth it out—then either plait it into one or two large plaits secured with scrunchies (*water catchers*) near the ends, or secure it in a ball at the back of my head with a scrunchie.

If you are just getting to know your hair, keep an eye on how you brush it. Brushing too hard may break your hair off. Experiment to find the "brushing balance" that works best for you. Stay away from the mythical figure of "200 brush strokes" a day. For tightly curled hair (or even permed hair) that can be a disaster.

The Afro

If I were to maintain my hair in its natural state and wear it loose on my head, I would have an Afro. The "Afro" is a hairstyle unique to African Americans. In its loose state, most African hair types tightly curl up and away from the scalp, creating a dome of the hair, the Afro. Not long ago I let a hairstylist "hard press" my natural hair. I was told that it would spring back to its natural state, but as my hair continued to grow out, I noticed that the old hair wasn't "springing back." (I may be partially to blame for this result. See the next section "Working with Hairstylists.") A large curl eventually returned to my hair texture, but it wasn't the small tight curl that was natural to my hair type. After letting my hair grow out for a few months, I ended up cutting out what I considered to be the bad hair (the hair that wasn't "springing back" to its full natural state).

From this experience, I learned two valuable lessons. One of them follows in the next section, "Working with Hairstylists." The other is detailed in the list below where I share how to work better with natural hair while wearing it in an Afro.

1. Never comb dry hair. Never go more than one week without

combing your hair. *If combing is difficult, trim your ends.*
2. **If you wash your hair at least weekly**, follow the steps outlined in the "Preparing Your Hair" section in "Step One: The Preparation." Use a wash-out conditioner during the washing process. Use a leave-in conditioner after the washing process.
3. **If you wash your hair more than once a week**, wash and condition your hair as you would if you were washing it weekly, BUT, do not comb your hair. Instead, after washing your hair and applying your leave-in conditioner, use your fingers to gently pull sections of your hair up and away from your scalp. You are doing this to help loosen and detangle your curls. During this process, you may notice those hairs that have been falling out due to the natural growth cycle of your hair, especially if your hair type is tight curls where the hair may fall out of your scalp, but not out of your hair until you comb your hair. I have noticed that these fallen hairs tend to congregate and form a ball around one strand so that it looks like a lot of hair has fallen out or broken off when I do comb my hair. I remind myself that I am seeing hairs that have fallen out due to the natural growth cycle of my hair, and hairs that have broken off during the washing process. It could also be an indication that I need to trim my ends.
4. After washing your hair following steps 2 or 3 above, place a silk or satin scarf over your head and gently pat your hair in order to give it a uniform look.

Take Note
To cut your Afro to one length/trim your ends, plait it in small even sections after a weekly washing. Cut a hard straw to the length that you want to trim your hair, or use some other tool that is already the length that you want to cut your hair. This is your cutting tool. As you unplait each plait, smooth the hairs up the length of your cutting tool, use your index finger and thumb of one hand to gather the hairs just above the length of the cutting tool. Use your other hand to cut these hairs just below the tip of your index finger and thumb. This keeps the ends trimmed, but I suggest that you work toward an overall *blunt cut* after your hair has grown out and you are able to

gather it into a ponytail at the nape of your neck. A blunt cut is easier to maintain, and better, I believe, for African hair types.

Working with Hairstylists

Hair like mine can be a handful to take care of when it is in its natural state, so after you have removed your braids for the final time and have allowed your hair to continue to grow in a loose state for some time, you may want to get it permanently straightened. When/if that time comes, you probably will be tempted to run, not walk, to your nearest hairstylist. Do your homework ahead of time. While you are still wearing your hair in braids, take note of other women's hair and ask them questions about where they get their hair done. If you like their answers, visit their salon, and make an appointment with the stylist in question.

Δ Try to let the hairstylist work with your natural hair for a few visits before you allow them to give you a perm. Who knows, you might be able to live with just getting your hair pressed, but if you get your hair permed right away, you'll never know that.

NOTE: A recent trend in working with natural hair seems to be pressing it so hard that it looks like your hair has been permed. Before you allow a hairstylist to hard press your hair, make sure that you communicate to the hairstylist that you do not want your hair to remain permanently straight (if that is your choice). In that regard, ask what products the hairstylist will use on your hair, how those products might affect your natural hair, and the temperature of the pressing instrument. One thing that may have caused my hair to not spring back to its natural state after getting it hard pressed may be my own fault. After I got home, I decided to drown my hair in an oil product to help it "shine" a bit more, and "stay straight" a little bit longer. To my chagrin, it did both. I will eventually get my hair pressed again, but next time I will be sure to ask for a "light," soft pressing, and afterward not overdo the use of oil on my hair.

After the initial appointment, it would be a good idea to ask yourself some questions: Did the stylist comb your hair the way you think it should be combed? If not, did you speak up, and, if it was necessary, share with the stylist how you'd like for her/him to comb your hair? Were you comfortable in the stylist's shop? Did you enjoy working with the stylist? Did you feel as though you could communicate freely with the stylist? Ask yourself, and the stylist, as many questions as you can think of before allowing the stylist that you have selected to work with give you a perm.

I remember that I once went to see a hairstylist who, for some strange reason, thought that it was okay to comb my hair as though she were attacking something. She used a hacking motion to comb my hair that, after a few minutes, had me wondering if I would have any hair left by the time she finished, so I politely asked for the comb (as respectfully, and privately, as I could), and proceeded to comb my hair as though it were the most precious thing in the world. When I finished, I handed the comb back to the stylist, and asked her to comb my hair as I had just combed it, which she did. At the time, my hair was long, and I wanted to keep it that way at least a little while longer, so I had to speak up.

Upon leaving the salon, I felt as though the stylist had respected my concerns, and that she did not get offended when I asked her to comb my hair a certain way. That is the type of person I look for to work with my hair. Of course, the hairstylist is the one with the professional training, but it's your head that she or he is working on, and remember, you're the one who has to see your reflection in the mirror every day.

The number one complaint that I hear over and over is that most hairstylists comb our hair by yanking it out. To be fair, our hair is not the easiest in the world to work with, and most hairstylists are working within a time constraint. Even so, look for hairstylists who will treat your hair as if it were the most precious thing in the world, and comb tangles out as I instruct in "Step One: The Preparation." Think from this perspective: If we don't treat our hair right, who will?

Some Things to Think About

In this chapter I have tried to stress that, as with any hairstyle, braided and natural hairstyles must be maintained. In realizing this, you are in a better position to avoid the myths that wearing your hair in its natural state or in braids will damage it or break it off. To reinforce what you've learned in my book, following is a chapter to recap everything titled "A Brief Recap."

Quick Thought Check #5

1. If you have no health issues, you should wash your hair no more than once a month.
   A. True
   B. False

2. To thicken up thin hair, you have to use a lot of false hair while braiding.
   A. True
   B. False

3. Hair should not be washed while wearing it in braids.
   A. True
   B. False

4. Hair should be rebraided on a monthly basis.
   A. True
   B. False

5. You should never experiment on your hair.
   A. True
   B. False

6. If you wear your hair in an Afro, you do not need to maintain it since you're wearing your hair in its natural state.
   A. True
   B. False

7. If you wear your hair in an Afro, you should only comb it when it is dry and not when it is wet.
   A. True
   B. False

QTC #5 Answers

1. The correct answer is "B," false. Please see page 72.
2. This answer here is also, "B," false. Please see page 44.
3. Again, the correct response is "B," false. Please see page 72.
4. The correct answer once again is "B," this is false. Please see page 72.
5. "B" is the correct answer. Please see page 37.
6. The correct answer is "B," false. Please see pages 78-79.
7. The correct answer to this statement is "B," false. Please see pages 33, 36, and 78.

Chapter 5
| A Brief Recap

Things to Remember
1. *Plan your time.* Schedule in on your calendar time to braid/rebraid your hair. If this is your first time braiding/rebraiding, plan at least eight hours for yourself so that you can take your time and study your hair as you work. It may not take you the entire eight hours, but even if it does, you are worth it!
2. ∆ *Keep your hair clean.* Wash and rebraid it at least once a week. Try not to go longer than two weeks without washing and rebraiding your hair. When not wearing braids, I'll usually wash my natural hair daily during the summer months, and weekly during the winter months. I have been known to wash it daily during the winter months, too, because I've found that combing my hair is easiest after washing it. If my hair is permed, it usually gets washed only once a week (two weeks maximum) by a hairstylist.
3. *Finger combing is not simply running your fingers through your hair as if they were a comb.* It involves moving your fingers through your hair in a motion similar to combing the hair with a comb, and also stopping to use your fingers to gently untangle your hair.
4. *Try not to let a hairstylist comb your long African hair type in the sink after washing it.* To comb our hair properly, a stylist should have us sit upright in their chair, and gently comb our hair from the ends up to the scalp. Remember to

take a change in shirts with you!
5. Δ *Remember that fiber puts weight on your hair.* A thick piece of fiber on a small slice of hair can cause breakage. This is especially important to remember if you decide to use fiber with thin hair or on a child's hair. Therefore, if you decide to use fiber, or wear long, thick braids, remember to take special notice of how your hair responds to the weight of the fiber.
6. Δ *Learn to notice what you are doing that may be breaking your hair off.* HALT and SUAH at home, and at the salon.
7. Δ *Use the CURB System.* Rubber bands can break your hair off if used improperly. Train yourself to use the CURB System in order to reduce hair loss and breakage that can be attributed to using rubber bands on your hair.
8. *Know what type of false hair you are using.* Try experimenting with using the different types to see which works best for you. When you unpack synthetic fiber you will usually find a large plait that is bound at both ends. The top is usually bound with a rubber band and a bobby pin. The free end is usually bound only with a rubber band. When you unpack human fiber, you will find that the hair is loose, being bound only at one end, usually by a gold spiral. I've always used synthetic fiber for braiding.
9. *Avoid using grease directly on your scalp.* It can clog the pores. For my thick, tightly curled hair, I've found that creamy-type leave-in conditioners are best to use.
10. *Prepare the fiber for your hair.* Wash fiber before you need to use it in the braiding process.
11. *Prepare your hair for braiding.* Start with clean hair and split-free ends. If your hair is straight, chemically or naturally, try wearing plaits for a few days before you plan to braid it so that the hair stands away from the scalp, which makes it easier to braid. You might also try plaiting your hair, washing it with the plaits in, and then allowing it to dry with the plaits in to achieve the same effect. Whenever I went from wearing my hair permed to wearing it in braids—that is if I didn't cut the perm out—I would try to let my hair grow out at least one half inch before I braided it.

Hair Braiding Tips

1. Remember to treat the fiber as if it were your hair. If you condition your hair with any type of conditioner, use that same condition on the fiber, too, and in the same manner.
2. Δ The closer your fingers are to your scalp while you braid your hair, the tighter the braid will be, the easier it is to insert the extension, and, usually, the more convincing it is that the extension is a part of your real hair. Remember to use caution, and as previously stated, never braid your hair so tightly that it is painful to smile and nod your head up and down and from side to side as this could eventually cause *permanent* hair loss.
3. Braid with your thumb, index, and middle fingers, and try holding the strands in your fists with the remaining fingers (sometimes the middle finger must also be used here) when they are not being braided.
4. To keep braids neat as you braid them, braid sections of hair from left to right if you're right-handed, or from right to left if you're left-handed.
5. When extending any of the styling methods discussed in this book remember to even the strands out after the extension has been added by taking from too-full strands and giving to not-so-full strands.
6. As you braid your hair, separate the strands through to the ends to keep them from bunching together.
7. Δ For greater control while braiding, I have found it a great help to hold the strands down to the braid/French braid with the left hand and separate the strands through to the ends with the right hand when going, for example, from step 2 to step 3 of the "As You Go" method of extending French braids.
8. Although learning how to braid your hair may seem easy, learning how to move your fingers, and how to use difficult hand motions as you braid your hair, may make learning how to braid your hair seem harder than it really is. Because I am right-handed, this book has been written from that point of view; however, if you are left-handed, try substituting

the word "left" when the sentence reads "right." Where this would be too difficult, and because the placement of the braids is important, I have included separate instructions for left-handed people.
9. Another good idea that I got from my sister is to use a cosmetologist's mannequin head to learn how to braid.

The Secret to Growing Longer Hair

On a ride home from college one weekend, a friend told me the secret to growing hair. She said that every time that you wash your hair, it grows.

At one time, I wore my hair in African braids for one and a half years. During that time I went from washing my hair about every two weeks to at least once a week, and while it was in braids, my hair grew from a little less than four inches to a little over twelve inches. When I took my braids out, I further tested my friend's theory and experimented by washing my hair daily, and at least for me, it seems to be true. I would take this a step further, and emphasize that the science behind this may simply be that nothing that is not supposed to, can grow in an unclean environment. Likewise, washing, for example, your hair daily after the environment that it grows in has changed from normal to dry may also hinder hair growth if you do not take steps to alleviate the changed environment (see hair oiling on page 77).

You have to experiment with your hair to find out for yourself what works for you, and what doesn't work for you. For example, I've had as many as five different bottles of shampoo and conditioner lining my shower walls at one time. The ones that didn't work for me, where I didn't like the feel of the product on my hair or how my hair behaved after I used them, I'd keep as backups to use for when I ran out of my favorite shampoo or conditioner.

Along those lines, I encourage you to wash your hair at least weekly while wearing it braided, and trim your split ends at least every few months. I usually trim my ends once every three to four months. If I'm having difficulty combing my loose hair after washing it, I know that my ends need to be trimmed. Without fail, after I trim my ends, I find it easier to comb my hair the next time I wash it, and I seem to lose fewer hairs.

Δ   When I'm not wearing braids, I'll usually wash my hair daily during the summer months and weekly during the winter months. If I wash my hair daily during the winter months, I'll make sure to cover my head with a satin scarf and cap before going outside, or if I have one, I'll use a cap with a satin lining. Even if I don't wash my hair daily during the winter months, I wear a cap to protect myself from the cold. Otherwise I'd be a regular at the doctor's office, trying to fight off a cold, or worse, pneumonia.

Also, remember to keep your comb and brush clean. Wash and condition your comb and brush at least weekly, using the same shampoo and conditioner that you use on your hair.

Maintaining a Healthy Head of Hair
I've read sources that state that human hair can have a growth cycle that is two to six years long, three to six years long, and other growth cycles. Likewise, I've read sources that state that within that time period, hair can grow anywhere from one-fourth of an inch in length, to one inch in length a month. At six inches a year on a six-year growth cycle that's 36 inches worth of growth. Measuring from the nape of the neck, that's hair long enough to almost sit on if you don't trim split ends periodically. Even so, the final length, of course, probably depends largely on your genetic makeup.

Barring genetic and medical reasons for hair not growing, the biggest culprit of no, or slow, hair growth may be ourselves. For example, if you trim your split ends every month, you may inadvertently be trimming away healthy length obtained during your growth cycle. So, if most of your hairs are on a two-year growth cycle, your hair may appear to not be growing. If you find that you need to trim split ends every month, you might want to take a look at what you are doing to your hair, and/or check with your doctor to see if there is a medical reason your ends seem to stay in a split state.

I have yet to learn how long my hair can grow, but as we discover our hair growth cycles, I believe that there are things that we can do to maintain healthy hair growth: keep your hair clean, exercise as your doctor recommends, keep your hair clean, eat healthy meals, keep your hair clean, comb and brush your hair with care, keep your hair clean, maintain split-free ends, keep your hair clean, regularly clean your comb and brush, and keep your hair clean.

Think of it like this: if you didn't bathe regularly, how long would it be before other people noticed? Keep your hair clean, and treat it with care. Unless your doctor says otherwise, wash your hair at least once a week.

Δ One final thing I'd like for you to consider in terms of growing your hair longer and maintaining hair growth: You can keep your split ends trimmed, protect your scalp, eat nutritious meals, HALT, SUAH, use the CURB System, and wash and condition your hair frequently, but it will all amount to a hill of beans if you don't admit to yourself that you want your hair to grow so that you can consciously comb your hair with care. If you snatch a comb through your hair, or force a comb through tangled ends, or over brush your hair (see "Brushing Your Hair Again" in "Step Three: Braid Care") then you might as well deliberately yank your hair out yourself.

Please comb and brush your hair as though it were something of value to you. Expect your hairstylist to do the same.

A Word About Exercising

I mentioned exercising as a way to help maintain a healthy head of hair, so I want to encourage you to consult with your doctor and exercise trainer before beginning any exercise routine. As for myself, I find speed walking to be a great way to lose weight or maintain a weight. I walk on a treadmill that has built-in bars that I can hold onto when necessary. Also, I'll usually swing my arms as I walk so that I feel like I'm getting a more complete workout.

I noticed a long time ago that some people only exercise what I consider to be the main part of the body, instead of the entire body. So, in addition to (or usually while) speed walking on my treadmill, I also do facial exercises. If I do the facial exercises while walking on the treadmill, I use the built-in bars of the treadmill to keep my balance as I walk.

Some Things to Think About

In summary, as we leave this chapter, please remember that consciously getting to know your hair and body is the best way to grow your hair longer and maintain a healthy head of hair. Don't be afraid to experiment with your hair. It will help you in the long run to grow, strengthen, and lengthen your hair over time.

Chapter 6
| A Bald-Headed Woman

The previous chapters in this book are instructive for learning how to use hair braiding to grow, strengthen, and lengthen your hair; in this chapter, I try to stress the importance hair plays in our society, and the fact that you are not alone in wanting your hair to grow longer, and you are not alone in wanting hairstylists to treat your hair as if it were the most precious thing on the Earth. Hair is important to most people. Consider that for many cultures around the world, hair is an extension of the human body, and is as important as any extremity.

I didn't realize just how important hair is until one day when I was living in Virginia, I cut my hair down to the scalp while learning to use clippers. It was an accident. It was during the hot summer months, so I couldn't hide beneath a scarf or a hat for very long periods of time, especially at work. I think I'd just moved back up to Richmond from my hometown and had been on a new job only a few months. The first day I cut my hair, someone at work thought that I just had my hair pulled back, but when she realized that I had cut my hair, she (though well-meaning) yelled out in surprise "Diana cut her hair!"

I knew this person to be a considerate individual, so I knew that she wasn't trying to embarrass me but was genuinely surprised. We had actually been classmates in the past while studying art in college, and we were surprised to find ourselves working for the same employer. I thought that it was funny that she was so surprised, and we had a good laugh; then I proceeded to explain to everyone that I was trying to cut out a perm that had gone bad (I'd been giving myself a perm about every six weeks). To make the cut efficient, I explained, I'd decided to use electric clippers. After all, how hard could it be to use them on myself?

Up until that time, I had never used electric clippers in my life. I wasn't sure that I really had the guts to cut my hair again, but I had thought to myself, *just make the first cut from down the middle of your head to the front, and then there's no turning back*. I was right, and my hair had never been shorter. Having no idea what I was doing, I'd selected a one-fourth inch guide comb to use. That size, I'd reasoned, would cut all of the perm out of my hair, and it would leave me with some hair. After the initial shock I eventually learned how to correctly work the clippers. Over time I started to cut my hair even shorter.

The hard part about having boyishly short hair came one day when I was standing in line at the 7-Eleven around the corner from my home. An obviously drunk customer—I can't remember if he was in front of me or behind me in the line—who held in his hands a bottle of liquor to purchase, looked straight at me and yelled out "A bald-headed woman!"

At first I was petrified and didn't know whether I wanted to yell something back at him or hit him in the face. He was a lot taller than me, but I figured he was drunk and would probably go down quick, and that would give me enough time to get away before he got back up.

But that was not to be. I had recently rededicated my life to Jesus Christ, and I was serious about my Christian walk. I had been baptized as a young girl, but since adulthood I had moved away from God, trying every way to "enlightenment" and the "truth" that I could find, before turning back to rediscover Christianity. Now I was putting dead things behind me, and I was serious about getting to know God.

As I stood there mortified, a strange thing happened. It was as if I could hear God saying to me: "**Yes you are bald right now, but so are women who don't have a choice, like those trying to recover from cancer.**" With those few words, God put things into perspective for me.

Back then I was anything but noble, but when I heard those

words, I knew that I didn't have to say anything to that man. I felt God put a peace, and a quiet confidence, in me with those words that I couldn't understand, but gladly accepted as His gift to me.

I shared this experience with some people at work, and they were so caring. It was like God confirming His words through their thoughtfulness.

Δ I guess I share that story with you now because should you choose a career in cosmetology, you might want to remember that you may never know what some of your clients have been through in their lives. Please comb everyone's hair as though it were of value, and respect that your clients' hair is their hair. You may have the best style planned for them, but if they don't like it, please don't get offended. Remember to respect that they are the ones who have to look in the mirror every day. And if in your career as a hairstylist you come across someone who has to wear a wig because their hair can no longer grow, do the same for them as you style their wig.

Cosmetology as a Career Choice

If this book has inspired you to take the next step and go to school to obtain a professional cosmetologist's license, then I encourage you to first take the time to get to know your own hair. Once you begin to understand what works, and what doesn't work for you, take the next step and try braiding someone else's hair. Remember that, without a business license, in many states you cannot charge someone to braid their hair.

Braiding someone else's hair will give you the opportunity to see if you would like to work with hair professionally. If you find yourself tapping someone on the head with your comb to remind them to sit still as you braid their hair, take it as a hint that cosmetology may not be the field for you. And you probably shouldn't try to braid anyone else's hair. Your sisters, brothers, and friends may not tap you back, but "real" people probably will hit you back, and hard.

Let's say that you pass the "braid someone else's hair" test. What do you do next? I recommend that you ask to shadow your favorite hairstylist for a few hours. That means that you simply tell them that you are thinking about becoming a professional hairstylist and would like to get a better understanding of the field by watching them for a few hours, or their entire work day. Shadowing is a career technique commonly used in the corporate world.

As you shadow them, remember that they are professionals, with obligations to patrons that must come first. However, this will be a learning experience for you, so be prepared with your questions, but remember to be polite, and respectful of their patrons' privacy.

If, after shadowing someone, you decide that you do indeed want to pursue a career as a professional cosmetologist, the next step would be for you to locate a school to attend. The person that you shadow will probably be able to help you in that regard, too. They may be willing to also mentor you as you make your way through school, and when you begin your career as a cosmetologist.

Cosmetologists seem to be becoming more and more the first line of defense for our health. For example, there have been incidents of hairstylists noticing subtle changes in the condition of their patrons scalps that have lead to timely diagnosis and treatment of diseases. In that regard, consider doing the following homework assignment. **HOMEWORK #3:** Visit the following links and read the information on Biotin concerning how it might affect medical testing for diseases.

- https://www.fda.gov/medical-devices/safety-communications/fda-warns-biotin-may-interfere-lab-tests-fda-safety-communication
- https://ods.od.nih.gov/factsheets/Biotin-Consumer/
- https://www.fda.gov/medical-devices/safety-communications/update-fda-warns-biotin-may-interfere-lab-tests-fda-safety-communication

Final Thoughts

I hope that each of the chapters within my book have given you some things to think about. What's on your head and in your heart, and how you choose to share it with others, matters.

You now have all of the tools that you will need in order to learn how to braid and grow your hair to longer lengths. I've said it before in this work, and it bears repeating: You are worth it!

Now you are ready to try hairstyles of your own. To assist you in this, following is a "Gallery of Hairstyles: Designs for Work, School, and Play." Contained within this chapter is "Your Personal Hair-Care Diary," which is a specially designed section for you to track what works for you and what doesn't as you learn how to use hair braiding to grow, strengthen, and lengthen your hair.

Chapter 7
| *Gallery of Hairstyles: Designs for Work, School, and Play*

This gallery not only gives the reader ideas for hairstyles, it also illustrates how to section and part the hair in order to achieve them. This aids the braider in learning how to read hairstyles worn by others, which may not be illustrated in this book, and apply them to her/his own hair.

To help the reader further understand how to read hairstyles, following the introduction to this chapter are illustrations of a slice, strip, strands, and the anatomy of a hairstyle. Whatever the braided style, remember to fit it to the setting. For example, at work, the focus is on getting the job done, so it's usually a good idea to wear conservative braided styles to work. On the other hand, if you're going out to a special dinner, for example, then the focus should be on you, and a more elaborate braided style would be in order (see page 61 subheading "Extending Plaits").

Slice, Strip, and Strands Illustrated

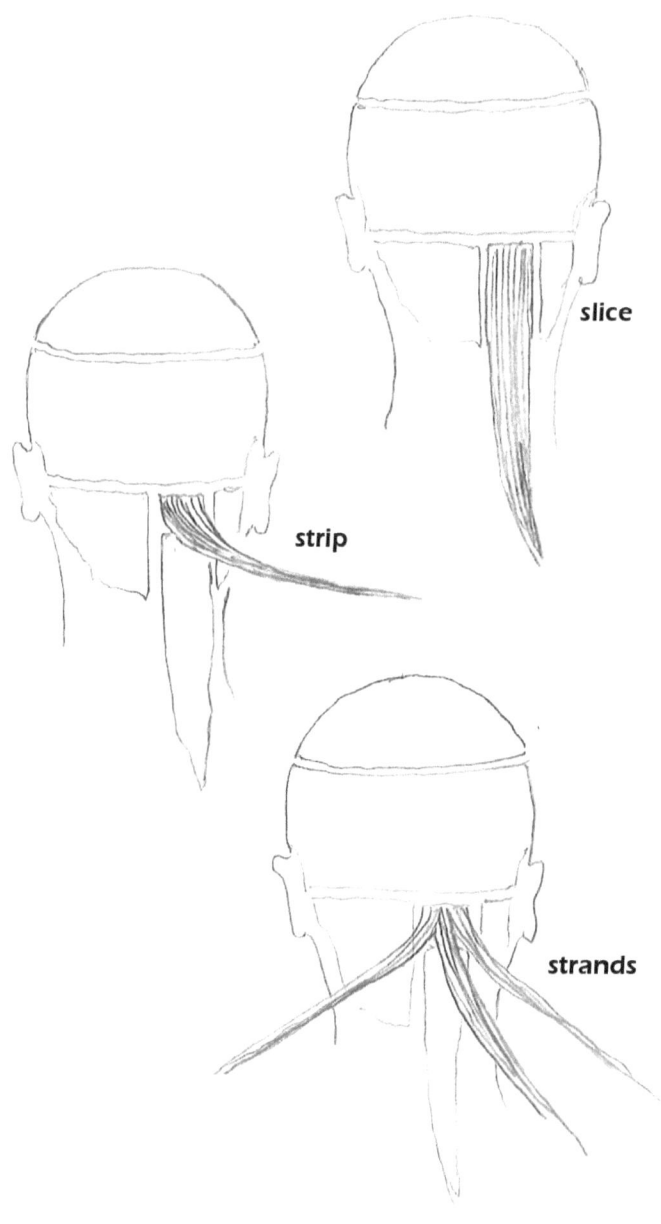

Chapter 7 | Gallery of Hairstyles: Designs for Work, School, and Play | 95

Slice, Strip, and Strands Explained

The slice, strip, and strands are the building blocks of braided hairstyles.

Small slices are usually used in African braiding, and larger slices are usually used in French braiding. Narrow-set braids (small slices) produce one tone, while wide-set braids (larger slices) produce another. Likewise, starting with a small strip of hair produces a tone different from when you start with a longer strip of hair.

Think of it like this, tone is that quality that makes things interesting. A song, for example, can be fast, or slow. A singer can sing high, or low. And, likewise, braided styles can be conservatively simple, or they can be variably complex.

HOMEWORK #4: Practice experimenting with tone. Work on this assignment by parting your hair in the back of your head.

1. Make two thin slices to work with. Vary the amount of hair that you pull from under/beneath each slice to make an African braid. Take very small amounts of the slice for one braid, and large amounts of the slice for the other braid. Do the same with two large slices of hair. Use a handheld mirror to view your handy work. Notice the differences between the slices. How can you use this styling technique to enhance your braids? Take these braids out.
2. Repart your hair in the back of your head so that you have one small slice of hair between two large slices of hair. African braid the large slices of hair so that they are the same tone. French braid the middle, smaller slice of hair using a small tone. Use a handheld mirror to review your handy work. How could you use this styling technique to style your hair in an elegant style suitable for an evening out?
3. Take these braids out one at a time and rebraid the larger slices as French braids, and the smaller slice as an African braid. Again review your handy work using a handheld mirror, and consider how, and for what purpose, you might use this styling technique.

Anatomy of a Hairstyle Illustrated: Hairstyle 1

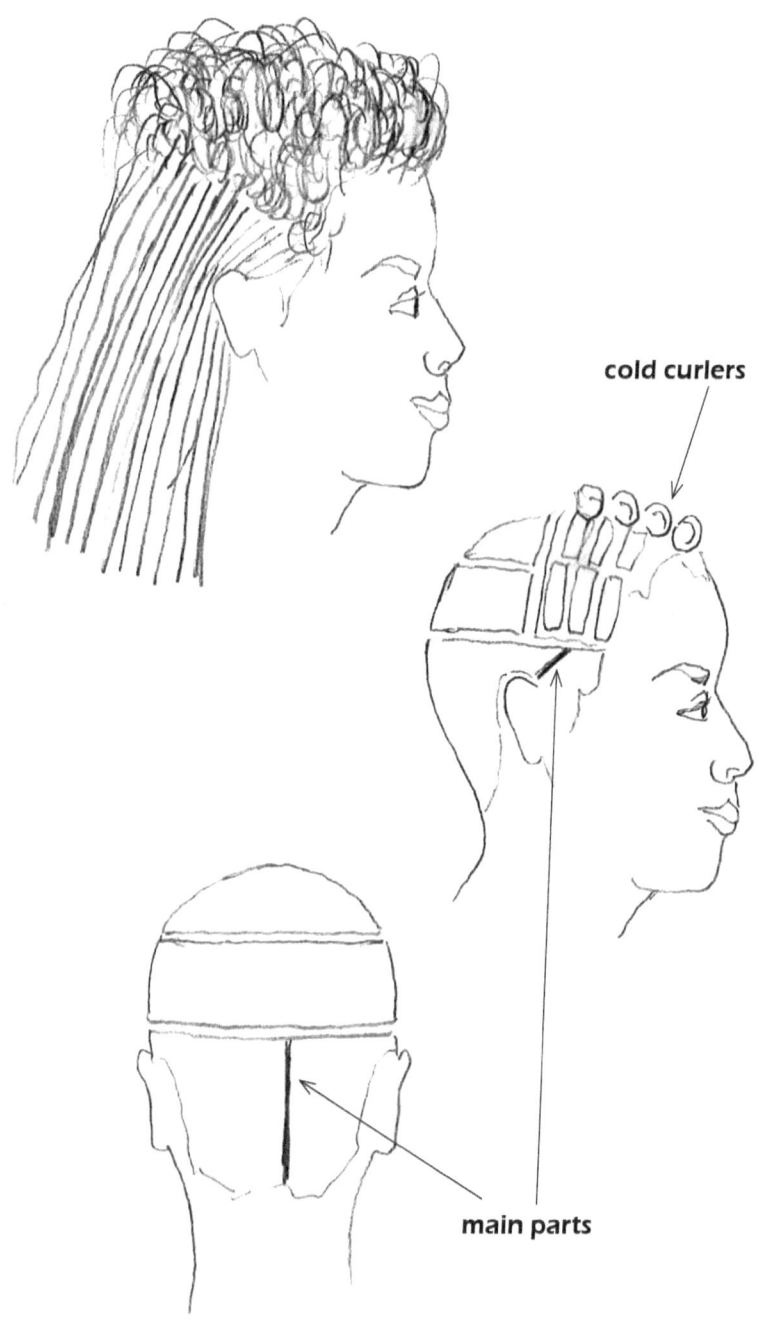

Anatomy of a Hairstyle Explained

On the opposite page, for **Hairstyle 1** you see:
1. A side view of the finished hairstyle, and side and back views of the blueprint for the hairstyle.
2. The main sections, of which there are four. The front section is curled in the finished style. During the braiding process, this hair is plaited out of the way. It is curled only after all braids have been completed. The side view of the blueprint has been illustrated with cold curlers that would be installed after the braiding process.
3. The main part for the side of the fourth section. It is slanted because all braids on the side are slanted.
4. The main part for the back section. Because the entire back is vertical, only one main part needs to be illustrated.

Hairstyle 2

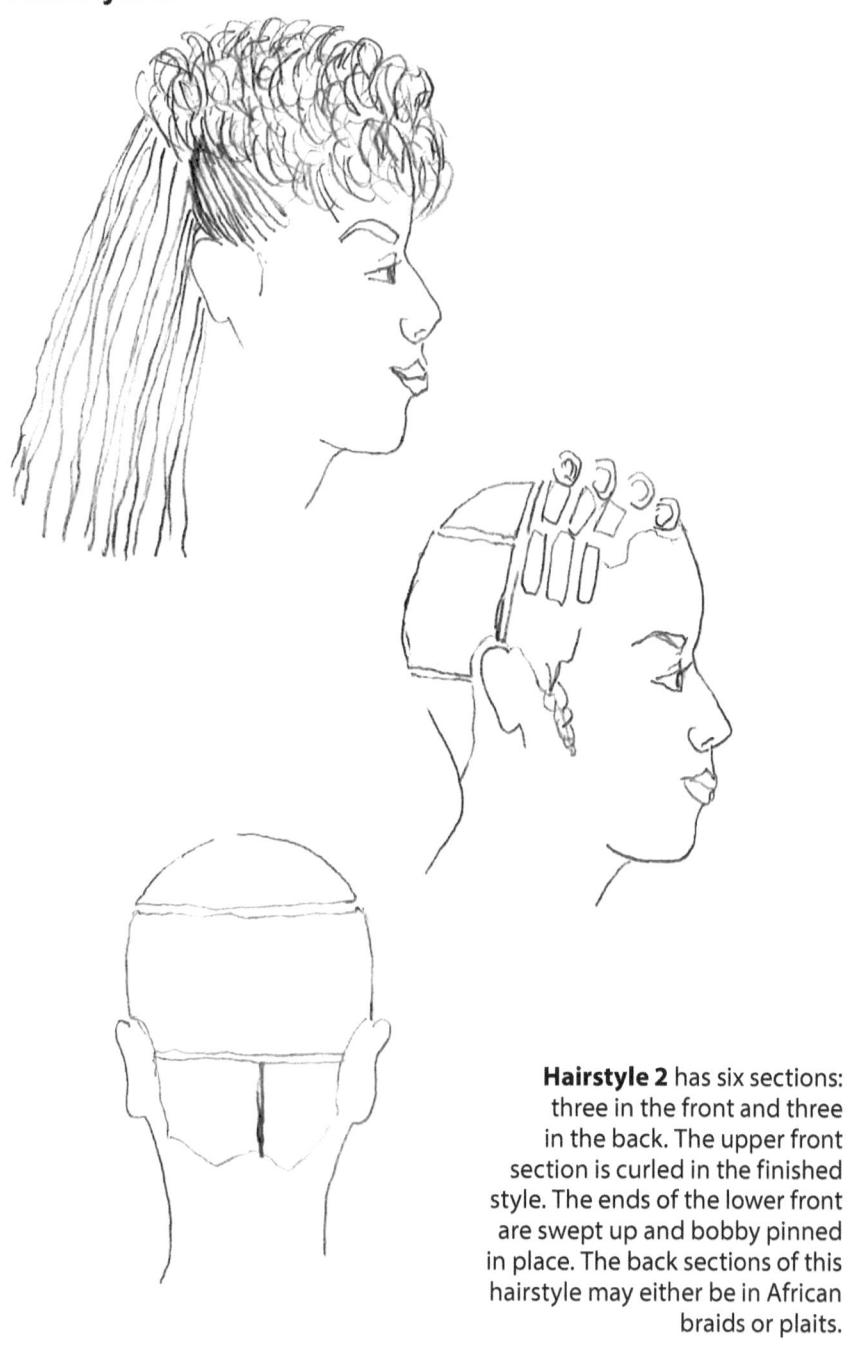

Hairstyle 2 has six sections: three in the front and three in the back. The upper front section is curled in the finished style. The ends of the lower front are swept up and bobby pinned in place. The back sections of this hairstyle may either be in African braids or plaits.

Hairstyle 3

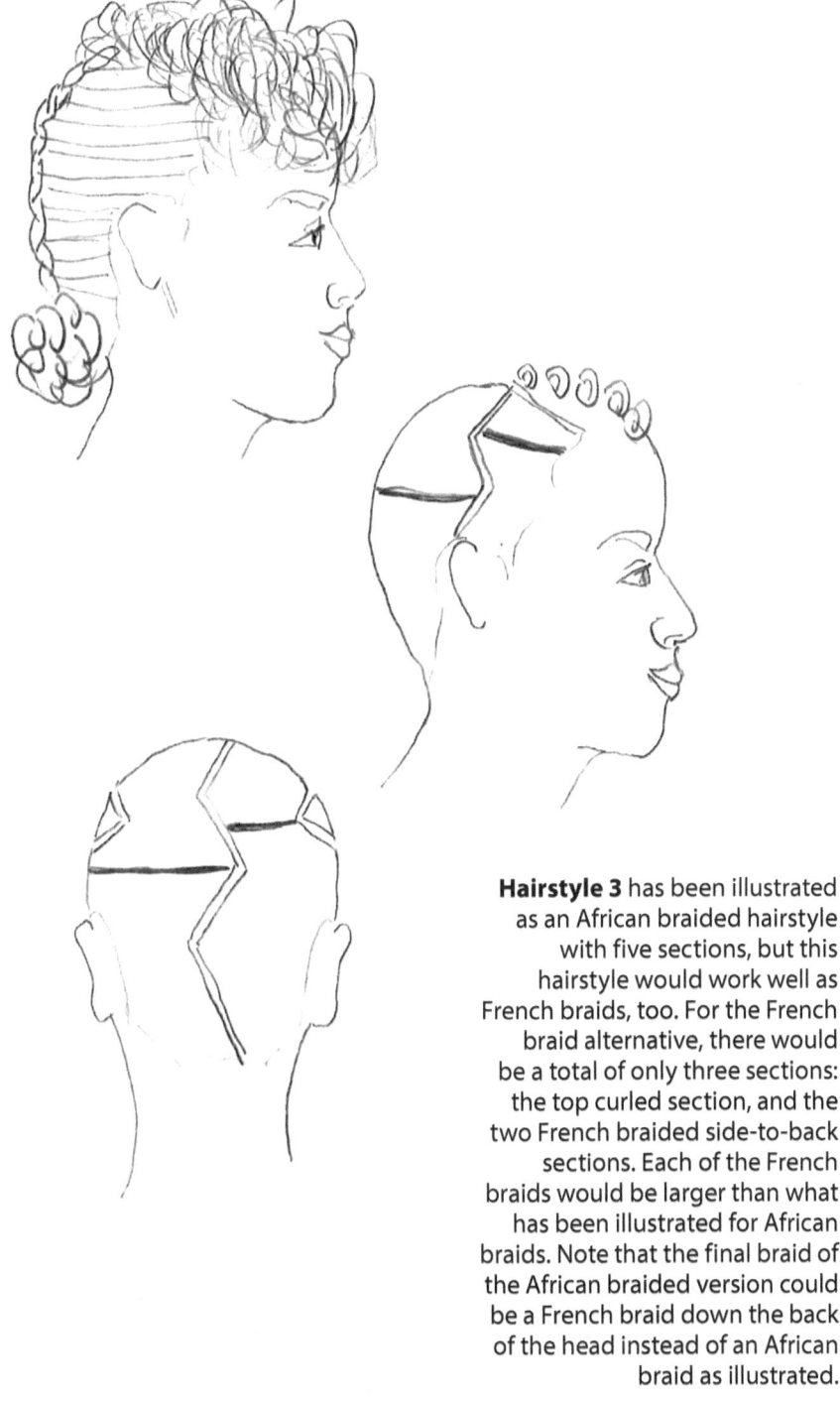

Hairstyle 3 has been illustrated as an African braided hairstyle with five sections, but this hairstyle would work well as French braids, too. For the French braid alternative, there would be a total of only three sections: the top curled section, and the two French braided side-to-back sections. Each of the French braids would be larger than what has been illustrated for African braids. Note that the final braid of the African braided version could be a French braid down the back of the head instead of an African braid as illustrated.

Hairstyle 4

Hairstyle 4 has five sections. This hairstyle is similar to the hairstyle (minus the bang) that I wore for one and a half years. The zigzag part on the top of the head has been exaggerated in the side view to give you a better idea of how the part should look. Only two parts on the top of the head make up the zigzag.

Hairstyle 5

Hairstyle 6

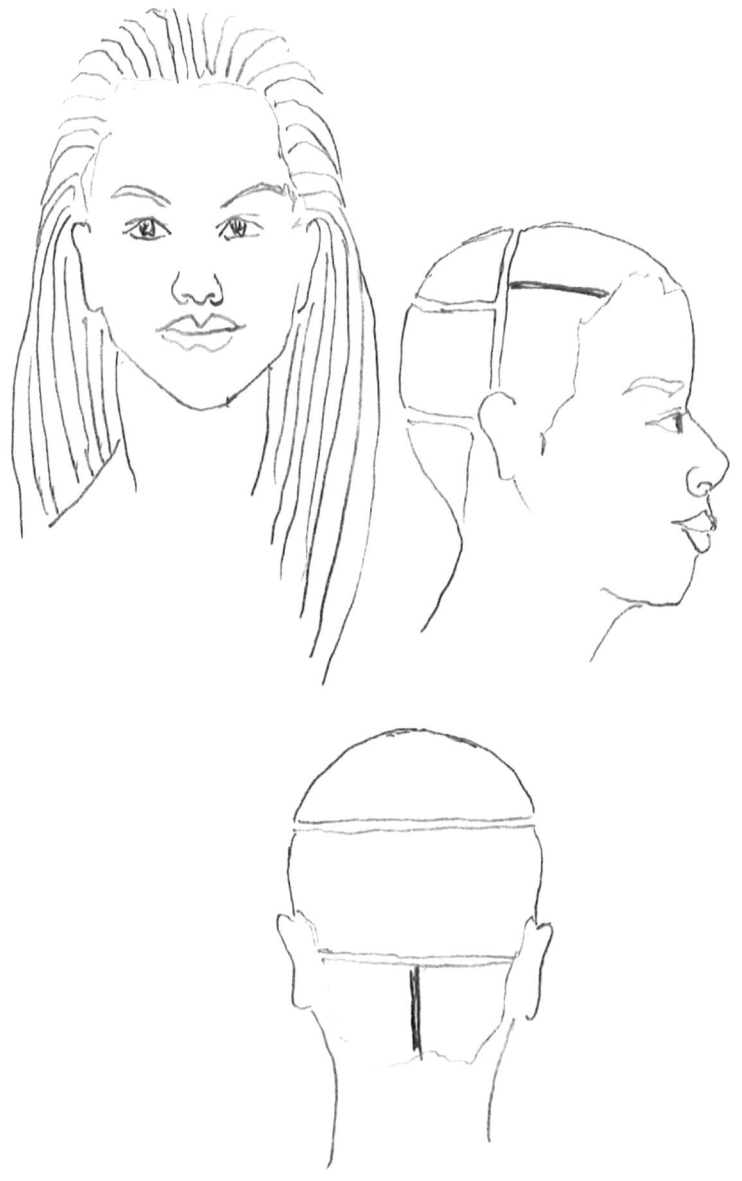

Hairstyle 7

Hairstyle 8

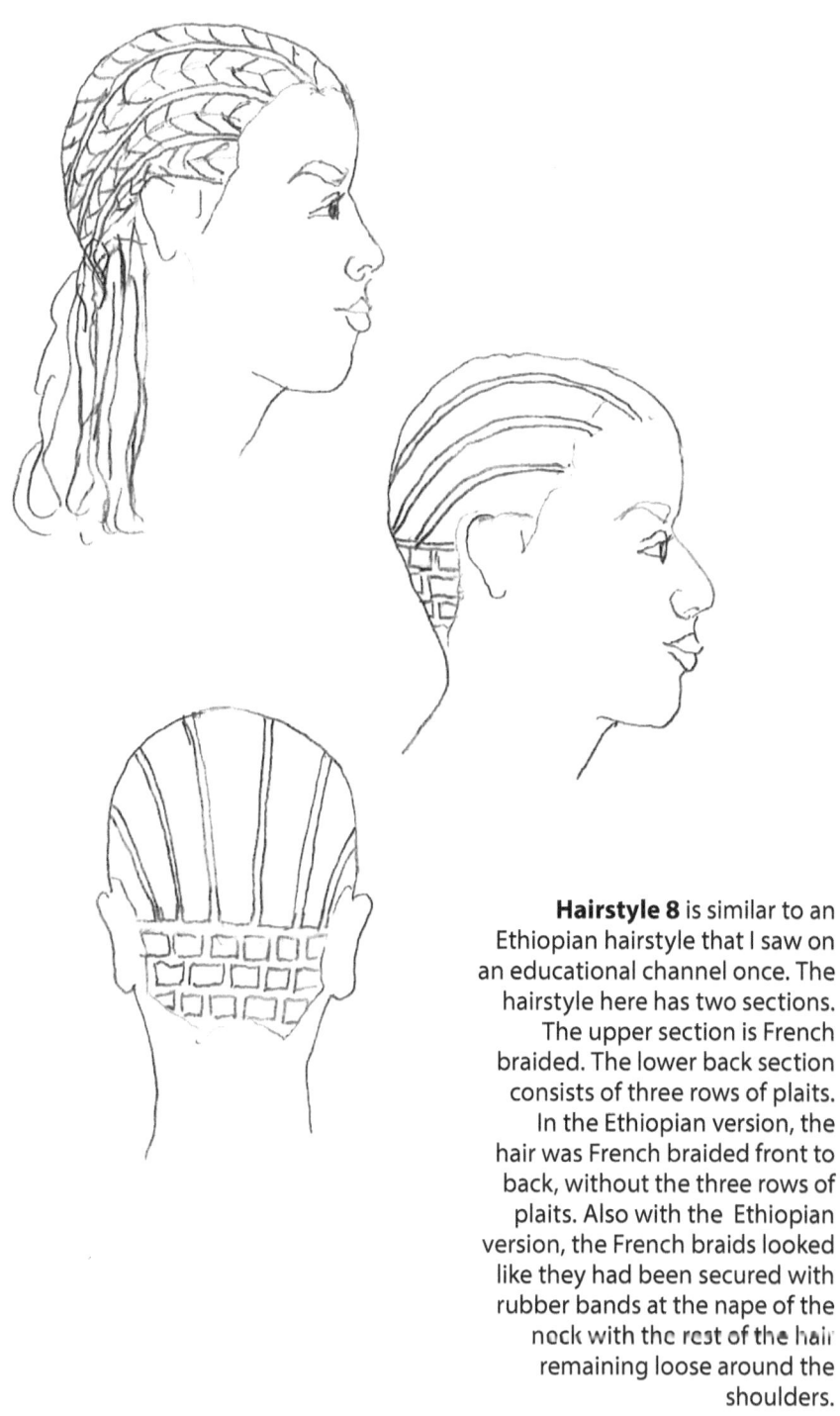

Hairstyle 8 is similar to an Ethiopian hairstyle that I saw on an educational channel once. The hairstyle here has two sections. The upper section is French braided. The lower back section consists of three rows of plaits. In the Ethiopian version, the hair was French braided front to back, without the three rows of plaits. Also with the Ethiopian version, the French braids looked like they had been secured with rubber bands at the nape of the neck with the rest of the hair remaining loose around the shoulders.

Hairstyle 9

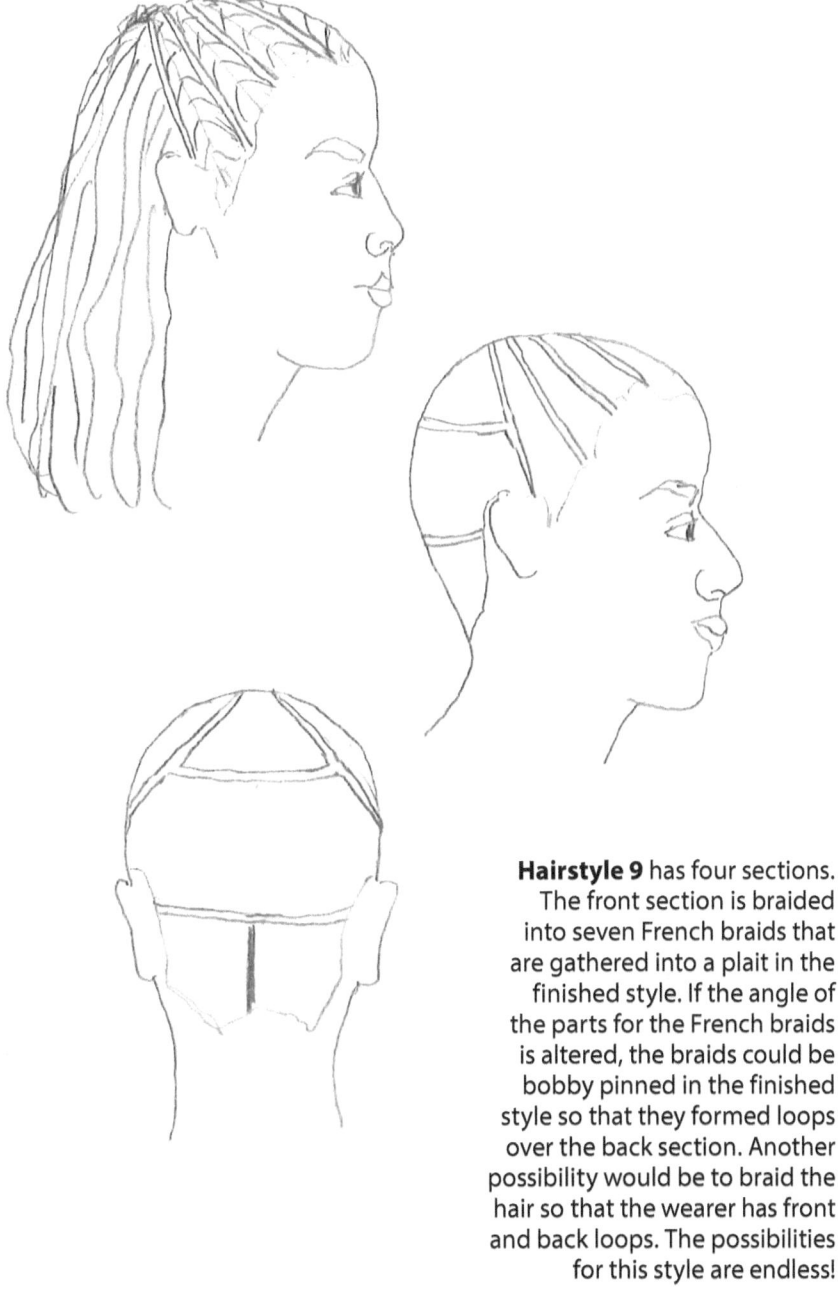

Hairstyle 9 has four sections. The front section is braided into seven French braids that are gathered into a plait in the finished style. If the angle of the parts for the French braids is altered, the braids could be bobby pinned in the finished style so that they formed loops over the back section. Another possibility would be to braid the hair so that the wearer has front and back loops. The possibilities for this style are endless!

The back three sections in the finished style may be either in braids, plaits, or remain loose.

Hairstyle 10

I added **Hairstyle 10** after the initial publication of my book. I had wanted an elegant hairstyle for a business-related dinner, and this is what I came up with for that evening. I was amazed at the wonderful comments I received on the hairstyle, both when I wore it to the dinner, and when I wore it to work the next day.

This hairstyle consists of nine French braids that run from the front to the back of the head, and one French braid in the middle of the back of the head. Once all French braids are in place, they are French braided together with the braid leaning to one side. The length of the final French braid is swept up underneath the braid to form a type of flat ball at the back of the head that's held in place with bobby pins.

A bang area is created in the front between the middle braid and either of the two braids on the sides of the middle braid. The bang area may either be plaited, as illustrated, to give a braided cascading effect, or left loose.

Quick Thought Check #6

1. You should braid your hair as tight as possible so that it stays neat as long as possible.
   A. True
   B. False

2. People who want their hair to grow are vain.
   A. True
   B. False

3. It doesn't matter how much fiber you use in a braid. The objective is to make your hair look good.
   A. True
   B. False

4. You should never use grease on your hair.
   A. True
   B. False

5. Braided hairstyles should not be worn in business settings.
   A. True
   B. False

6. You should only comb your hair when it is wet.
   A. True
   B. False

QTC #6 Answers

1. False. Braiding the hair too tight can eventually cause the wearer to lose hair on the area of the scalp where the hairs have been braided too tight. Please see pages 40, and 85.
2. This is false. Please see pages 89-91.
3. The correct answer is "B," false. Please see pages 44-45, and 84.
4. "B" is the correct answer. Please see pages 34, 75, and 84.
5. The answer is "B," false. Please see pages 27, 69, and 106-107.
6. This correct answer is "A," true. Please see pages 33, and 78.

Your Personal Hair-Care Diary

Keeping records is a tool to help monitor growth and development in any area of study. Use the following pages to sketch your own hairstyles, keep a record of your progress from month to month, and make notes on what works for you and what doesn't work for you.

How to Use Your Hair-Care Diary

Your diary consists of three calendar pages that you will need to fill in with year and date information, three pages for note-taking, and seven pages on which to sketch the anatomy of new hairstyles that you would like to try out. The calendar pages are for you to record recurring activities such as when you trim split ends, for example. The idea is not to pre-record information, but to color-code your calendars, based on the colors that you have chosen in your legend for each activity, as you execute each activity. This will help you to gain a better idea of when you actually perform each activity.

For example, if you have color-coded "washed hair, trimmed ends and rebraided" green in "Your Color-Coded Legend," and decide to do all of that on January 26, 2019, then that date would be entered onto your calendar, and the square for that date would be colored all green (or you could put a green dot on that date) on your calendar. In the corresponding milestone notes section, you might note that your hair was unusually difficult to comb on that date, so you trimmed your split ends. You could also record how your hair combed before and after the trim, and the length of your hair post-trim as well. Between the calendars and your milestone notes, over time you may see patterns emerge that can help you to make better decisions regarding when, for example, to trim your split ends.

Calendar Example

January 20 19
S	M	T	W	T	F	S
		1				
						12
					26	
		31				

February 20 19
S	M	T	W	T	F	S
					1	
						16
				28		

March 20 19
S	M	T	W	T	F	S
					1	
31						

April 20 19
S	M	T	W	T	F	S
	1					
	30					

May 20 19
S	M	T	W	T	F	S
			1			
			31			

June 20 19
S	M	T	W	T	F	S
						1
30						

July 20 19
S	M	T	W	T	F	S
	1					
			31			

August 20 19
S	M	T	W	T	F	S
				1		
					31	

September 20 19
S	M	T	W	T	F	S
1						
	30					

October 20 19
S	M	T	W	T	F	S
		1				
			31			

November 20 19
S	M	T	W	T	F	S
					1	
					31	

December 20 19
S	M	T	W	T	F	S
1						
30						

Your Color-Coded Legend:

- ☐ trimmed split ends
- ☐ washed hair
- ☐ deep conditioned hair
- ☐ rebraided hair
- ☐ washed hair, trimmed ends and rebraided hair

Milestone Notes Example

2019

Date	Time Begin	Time End	Total	Activity/Comment
2/16	3p	11p	8h	washed hair, trimmed ends & rebraided hair
2/28	6p	11:30p	5h 30m	took braids out completely; hair has grown about three inches since 11/1/2018

Year One Calendar

January						20
S	M	T	W	T	F	S

February						20
S	M	T	W	T	F	S

March						20
S	M	T	W	T	F	S

April						20
S	M	T	W	T	F	S

May						20
S	M	T	W	T	F	S

June						20
S	M	T	W	T	F	S

July						20
S	M	T	W	T	F	S

August						20
S	M	T	W	T	F	S

September						20
S	M	T	W	T	F	S

October						20
S	M	T	W	T	F	S

November						20
S	M	T	W	T	F	S

December						20
S	M	T	W	T	F	S

Your Color-Coded Legend:

Chapter 7 | Gallery of Hairstyles: Designs for Work, School, and Play | 113

Year One Milestone Notes

Date	Time Begin	End	Total	Activity/Comment

Year Two Calendar

January	20
S M T W T F S	

February	20
S M T W T F S	

March	20
S M T W T F S	

April	20
S M T W T F S	

May	20
S M T W T F S	

June	20
S M T W T F S	

July	20
S M T W T F S	

August	20
S M T W T F S	

September	20
S M T W T F S	

October	20
S M T W T F S	

November	20
S M T W T F S	

December	20
S M T W T F S	

Your Color-Coded Legend:

Year Two Milestone Notes

Date	Time Begin	End	Total	Activity/Comment

Year Three Calendar

January	20

S	M	T	W	T	F	S

February	20

S	M	T	W	T	F	S

March	20

S	M	T	W	T	F	S

April	20

S	M	T	W	T	F	S

May	20

S	M	T	W	T	F	S

June	20

S	M	T	W	T	F	S

July	20

S	M	T	W	T	F	S

August	20

S	M	T	W	T	F	S

September	20

S	M	T	W	T	F	S

October	20

S	M	T	W	T	F	S

November	20

S	M	T	W	T	F	S

December	20

S	M	T	W	T	F	S

Your Color-Coded Legend:

☐ _____

☐ _____

☐ _____

☐ _____

☐ _____

Year Three Milestone Notes

Date	Time Begin	End	Total	Activity/Comment

Your Hairstyles and Notes

Your Hairstyles and Notes

Your Hairstyles and Notes

Your Hairstyles and Notes

Your Hairstyles and Notes

Your Hairstyles and Notes

Your Hairstyles and Notes

Glossary

Following are definitions for words as used in this book that are unique to this book.

Δ: This symbol is the fourth letter of the Greek alphabet, the Delta. It is represented here in the uppercase. In science and math, it is used to represent change. Hence its use in this book. When you see this symbol, remember to use less force (change—lessen—the amount of force you would normally use) on the hair.

–*A*–

African braiding: The process of plaiting the hair down to the scalp by using the underhand method of plaiting the hair, and including hair from the side/beneath of a slice.

Afro: A hairstyle unique to African Americans where natural hair has been cut to one length, usually, and is worn loose on the head, creating a dome of the hair. A variation of this hairstyle is to bind the hairs near the scalp with some type of a band and allow the hairs in the band to remain loose at the ends, forming an Afro puff. Body straight and bone straight hair types imitate the Afro by first curling the hair, and then teasing it near the scalp with a fine-toothed comb so that the hairs tangle in order for the hair to appear to stand up and away from the scalp. Teasing the hair simply means that you select a stand of hair, place the comb in the hair near the scalp as if you were going to comb the hair, and then simply move the comb up and down the strand so that the hairs tangle near the scalp.

–*B*–

Base: At the scalp, where the roots of the hair grow out from the scalp.

Blunt cut: A blunt cut is a way to cut the hair so that it appears to be all one length when it lays flat against the scalp. The hair is measured from the top of the head to the ends of the hair, and then cut straight across at the desired length. All of the hairs on the head then look to be one length, but if each hair were pulled away from the scalp, it could be observed that each hair is really a different length when measured from the scalp to the end of the hair.

Bottom of the slice: Where African braiding or French braiding ends and plaiting begins.

Bound end(s): Refers to how fiber is packaged. Synthetic fiber is bound at the top and bottom; the top is the bound end, and the bottom is the free end. Human fiber is usually bound only at the top, the free end being loose.

Braid(s), braided, braiding, braiding process: Used interchangeably in this book. Depending on the context of the sentence, it can refer to African braids, French braids, plaits, or extensions, as opposed to simply braids.

Buildup: A combination of dust, natural scalp oil, grease, sweat, dead skin cells, lint, etc., which can combine to weaken and damage hair. Buildup also can cause matting. In addition, buildup can cause an almost unbearable itching on the scalp, which is an indication that the hair needs to be washed. Buildup occurs most heavily near the base.

–C–

Clippers: Electric scissors used for cutting the hair along the contours of the scalp.

Cornrows: This term and the term braids are used interchangeably as they both generally refer to the same hairstyling method.

CROWN Act, The: CROWN is an acronym that stands for "Creating a Respectful and Open Workplace for Natural hair." SB 188 was signed into California law by Gov. Gavin Newsom on Wednesday, July 3, 2019. It was championed by state Sen. Holly Mitchell, and is the first statewide protection in the United States that bans discrimination against the natural hair of African Americans. The bill was published in California on July 4, 2019. As of this writing, only New York City has enacted a similar bill.

CURB System: Correctly Using Rubber Bands System. This is the system invented by my sister to reduce hair breakage and hair loss that can be attributed to incorrectly using rubber bands on the hair.

Curly perm: One of two types of chemical treatments that African Americans might use on their hair. The term refers to hair that has been permanently curled a specific diameter. This is achieved by using a chemical solution on the hair and curling the hair with plastic (cold) hair curlers. At the end of the process, the hair that has been curly permed will not revert to its original curl state. The diameter of the curl is based on the diameter of the cold curler used on the hair during the chemical process. The other type of chemical treatment is known as a perm.

Cut bulk: Fiber that has been cut to a desired length in preparation for braiding.

–E–

Earlines: The line areas between the skin above and behind your ears and the hairs on your scalp.

Extensions: Fiber that has been interwoven into real hair.

–F–

Fiber: All false hair, whether synthetic or human.

Free end(s): The bottom of the length of fiber or hair.

French braid: The process of plaiting the hair down to the scalp by using the overhand method of plaiting the hair and including hair from the sides of a slice.

–H–

Hair types: In most cultural groups, different hair types can be found. For example, hair types among African Americans vary from, and may be a combination of, curly, straight, or wavy hair. These hair types are defined in this book as: *loose curls*, which refers to hair in which the diameter of the curls is one-fourth inch or larger; *tight curls*, which refers to hair in which the diameter of the curls is less than three-sixteenths of an inch, and the individual hairs form a tight coil that sometimes reverses into a half curl along the length of the hair; ***body straight***, which refers to hair that has a slight curl near the scalp, but other than that curl, the hair grows straight; ***bone straight***, which refers to hair that has no body whatsoever, or potential for a natural curl; and/or, ***loose or tight waves***, which refers to hair that does not actually curl, but appears to alternately half-curl in one direction and then the opposite direction (in the shape of an "S") with the free ends of the hair (usually) appearing to actually curl. Wavy hair may half-curl either side to side, where the hairs lie flat on the scalp; or, the hair may appear to half-curl up and down, where the hairs stand up and away from the scalp.

Hair-esteem: I began using this term to describe the overall feeling of feeling good about your hair after publishing the first edition of my book when I began to realize that we need good, healthy hair-esteem as much as we need a healthy self-esteem. This includes reconsidering, and abandoning the use of, old terminology developed from a negative perspective of black hair, like the word "kinky."

Hairline: The line area between the skin on your face and the hairs on your scalp. Depending on the context of the sentence, hairline can refer to all line areas: hairline, earlines, and neckline.

HALT: Hair and Lines Test. A test to perform on yourself to see if you are causing hair breakage along your hairline, earlines, or neckline. The test simply requires that you take notice of how you wash, and dry the line areas of your hair. You are checking to see if you are catching the length of your hair between the neckline area (for example) and your wash cloth or towel as you wash or dry the back of your neck, which could cause hair breakage as a result.

–K–

Kinky: This word generally refers to anything abnormal, weird, bizarre, deviant in behavior, etc. NOTE: I believe that using this word to describe an African American hair type as kinky hair may subliminally enforce negative stereotypes, low self-esteem, and negative self-image.

–L–

Line areas: If you were to take a black marker and draw a line around your head where the hair on your scalp stops and your skin begins, you would have marked the following areas: the area between the skin on your face and the hairs on your scalp (hairline), the area between the skin on the back of your neck and the hairs on your scalp (neckline), and the areas between the skin above and behind your ears and the hairs on your scalp (your earline areas).

Locs, locks: This is a hairstyle that originated with Rastafarians. It has been refined by African Americans. The original hairstyle was called dreadlocks (please see the NOTE on Kinky concerning kinky hair). The history of how the dreadlock hairstyle came to be is interesting, as is the Ras Tafari name, but it will not be covered in this book. In the Rastafarian version, individual hairs are allowed to tangle and grow in long, uncontrolled strands, resulting in a hairstyle where some strands are thicker than other strands. In the African American version of this hairstyle, hair is grown out in a controlled fashion. The hair, as in the Rastafarian version, is deliberately allowed to tangle so that it "locks" up to the point that it cannot be easily untangled, and combed. In the African American version, the hair is deliberately parted into small sections similar to small plaits, and then it is deliberately rolled and twisted between the fingers to help the hair begin to lock. An even more refined version of locs, which was developed by Dr. JoAnne Cornwell, is called "Sisterlocks®."

–M–

Main part: Braided styles may be slanted, horizontal, or perpendicular to the wearers' shoulders. Main sections are subdivided during the braiding process to insure that the braids of the section being braided either slant, or are straight up and down—for example, to achieve the desired effect of the chosen style. This is usually accomplished by the strategic placement of one or more main parts.

Main sections: All braided styles can be sectioned off for volume (layers) or more control during the braiding process. These sections are then plaited or bobby pinned out of the way while the braider works on one section at a time.

Matted, matting: When braids have been in for some time without rebraiding, especially plaits, they may begin to look like a hairstyle called *locs* (can also be spelled as *locks*) that is worn by some Rastafarians. The appearance is that the hairs of the braid or plait seem to grow as one piece, or strand, of hair.

–N–

Nappy hair: Uncombed, or severely tangled hair.

Natural hair: Hair that has not been chemically altered (permed) or pressed.

Neckline: the line area between the skin on the back of your neck and the hairs on your scalp.

–O–

Overhand plaiting: A method of styling the hair whereby a lock of hair is separated into three strands. The left or right strand is twisted over the center strand. The third strand is then similarly twisted with the center strand. The process is then repeated. This method of plaiting the hair is the basis of all French braided hairstyles.

–P–

Perm, permanent, permed: One of two types of chemical treatments that African Americans might use on their hair. The hair is permanently straightened (permed) by using a chemical solution so that it will not revert to its original state. The other type of chemical treatment is known as a curly perm.

Plait: A method of styling the hair whereby a lock of hair is separated into three strands. Two adjacent strands are then either twisted over or under each other. The third strand is then similarly twisted with the center strand. The process is then repeated. Twisting the strands over each other is known as overhand plaiting. Twisting the strands under each other is known as underhand plaiting.

Press, pressing: The hair is temporarily straightened (pressed) using a special metal comb, heat, and a pressing creme or hair grease. Soft pressed hair retains some of the look and feel of its natural texture. Hard pressed hair does not, and looks like the hair has been chemically treated to keep it permanently straight.

–R–

Retouch, retouching: When a perm is applied to the hair, its effects are permanent only on the hair on which the perm is applied. To keep the hair consistent in hair type, and to avoid breakage, a new perm is applied, based on the manufacturer's suggestions, to any hair that has grown out since the initial/last perm. This is called retouching the hair.

–S–

Scrunchies: Fabric covered elastic.

Seam ripper: This is a sewing instrument used by seamstresses/tailors to remove (rip) stitches from fabric. In braiding, it is used with the CURB System.

Shears: small scissors used to cut hair to a certain length or to trim the ends of the hair.

Slice: Refers to the hair to be braided, as in the hair between two parallel parts, or the hair between the hairline and a part parallel to it.

Strand(s): In braiding, the strip is usually divided into three parts; each part is considered one strand.

Strip: The initial lock of hairs that are separated from the slice in preparation for braiding. When plaiting the hair, the strip and the slice are usually one and the same.

SUAH: Smooth Up and Hold. A system used to prevent hair breakage while bathing and drying off. Hair is smoothed up and away from a line area and held in place with one hand as you use your wash cloth or towel with the other hand along the line area. NOTE: A hair band would work as well.

–T–

Tight curls/Tightly curled hair: The hair type that is frequently, and incorrectly, referred to as kinky hair. This hair type has a tight, coil-type structure that sometimes reverses into a half curl along the individual hairs.

Too tight: Hair that has been braided too close to the scalp. Over time, hair that has been repeatedly braided too tightly may cause hair loss in the area.

Trim: To cut one-fourth inch to one-half inch from the ends of your hair.

–U–

Underhand plaiting: A method of styling the hair whereby a lock of hair is separated into three strands. The left or right strand is twisted under the center strand. The third strand is then similarly twisted with the center strand. The process is then repeated. This method of plaiting the hair is the basis of all African braided hairstyles.

–W–

Wash: To shampoo and condition the hair, or the tools used on the hair, such as combs, picks, and brushes.

Water catchers: Scrunchies that have been wrapped around the ends of freshly washed and plaited hair in order to catch water so that it does not drip from the ends of the plait onto the wearer.

Wean: To slowly stop using hair grease on the scalp.

Quick Thought Check #7

1. What does this "Δ" symbol mean?

2. You should braid your hair as tight as possible so that it stays neat as long as possible.
   A. True
   B. False

3. To thicken up thin hair, you have to use a lot of false hair while braiding.
   A. True
   B. False

4. SUAH means:
   A. Stand Up And Holla
   B. Sit Up and Hear
   C. Smooth Up and Hold

5. Braids should not be worn in a business setting.
   A. True
   B. False

6. If you wear your hair in an Afro, you do not need to maintain it.
   A. True
   B. False

7. If you run into resistance combing wet hair, you should wet the comb, not your hair, and then continue detangling your hair.
   A. True
   B. False

QTC #7 Answer

1. Please see pages xiv, and 125 for the answer to this question.
2. False. Please see pages 40, and 85.
3. This answer here is also, "B," false. Please see pages 44-45, and 84.
4. "C" is the correct answer. SUAH is an acronym that stands for Smooth Up and Hold. Please see page 36.
5. False. Please see pages 27, 69, and 106-107.
6. The correct answer is "B," false. Please see pages 78-79.
7. This answer is "A," true. Please see page 35.

Further Reading and Study

This book is autobiographical in nature, and represents my attempt to share with the reader my knowledge of, and experiences with, hair braiding. Nonetheless, there are some references that I'd like to share that I came across while researching the magazine articles that were an influence on me.

Unless otherwise noted in the text of this book, the following have not been used as references for this book; I've listed them for your information because they all contain information that might help you to become a better braider, give you some insight into African American culture, or help you to grow as a Christian.

Books, Magazines, Multimedia, and Newspaper Articles

Translations of the Bible that I like to study from include the:
- King James Version (KJV)
- New American Standard Bible (NASB), and
- New Revised Standard Version (NRSV)

Akbari, Lisa. *The Black Woman's Guide to Beautiful Hair: A Positive Approach to Managing Any Hair and Style.* Naperville, IL: Sourcebooks, 2002.
A glance at Akbari's table of contents reveals an interesting chapter titled "Your Mind."

Bahney, Jennifer Bowers. *Longhairlovers®: Healthy Hair Secrets Revealed.* 2nd ed. Columbus, OH: Longhairlovers.com, 2014.
Bahney has an interesting section on seven sisters who became famous for their long hair, the Sutherland Sisters of Lockport, New York.

Banks, Ingrid. *Hair Matters: Beauty, Power, and Black Women's Consciousness.* New York: New York University Press, 2000.

Byrd, Ayana D. and Lori L. Tharps. *Hair Story: Untangling the Roots of Black Hair in America.* New York: St. Martin's Press, 2001.

Campbell, Barbara. 1973. "Melba? She's the Toast of the Town." *The New York Times*, February 18, 1973. https://www.nytimes.com/1973/02/18/archives/melba-shes-the-toast-of-the-town-melba-tolliver.html.
This link leads to an article on Melba Tolliver.

"Campus Queens." 1975. *Ebony*, April 1975.

"Corporate Dress Codes Can Turn Hair-Raising." 1988. *Chicago Tribune.* March 28, 1988. https://www.chicagotribune.com/news/ct-xpm-1988-03-28-8803040632-story.html.
This link leads to an article on Cheryl Tatum.

gibson, aliona l. *nappy: Growing Up Black and Female in America.* New York: Harlem River Press, 1995.
This book has a wonderful chapter on the author's relationship with her hair and her self-image. I love that she had an experience similar to my own when she cut her hair short. It helped me to realize that I was not alone in my struggle to accept my natural hair, as I simultaneously learned not to allow the ignorance of others to define my worth, or my self-esteem.

Hilbring, Veronica. 2018. "10 Black Women News Anchors Who Paved The Way In Broadcast Journalism." *Essence.* January 4, 2018. https://www.essence.com/news/black-women-news-anchors-broadcast-journalists/. This link leads to an article that includes information on Melba Tolliver.

James, Duyan. Hairtalk: *Stylish Braids from African Roots.* New York: Sterling Publishing Co., Inc., 2007.

Kingsley, Philip. *The Hair Bible: A Complete Guide to Health and Care.* Kindle ed. London: Aurum Press Ltd., 2014.

Lasky, Kathryn. *Vision of Beauty: The Story of Sarah Breedlove Walker.* 2nd ed. Somerville, MA: Candlewick Press, 2012.
This is a picture book for young children about the story of Madam C. J. Walker, an African American who became **the first female millionaire** by manufacturing and marketing her own hair care products.

Majette, Susan. *When Reality Shines.* rev. ed. Chesapeake, VA: Kabod Publishing, 2008.
Written by the cousin of one of my cousins, this is an interesting book about surviving systemic lupus erythematosus, which includes how the author dealt with hair loss due to that disease.

Malcolm X. *The Autobiography of Malcolm X: As Told to Alex Haley.* New York: Ballantine Books, 2015.

Norment, Lynn. 1979. "Peaches and Herb: They take a trip to the top the second time around." *Ebony,* June 1979.

Rock, Chris. *Good Hair: Sit Back and Relax.* DVD. Directed by Jeff Stilson. Lions Gate Films, 2009.

Schachter, Jim. 1988. "EEOC Says Hyatt Showed Bias in Its Ban on Cornrows." *Los Angeles Times.* May 17, 1988. https://www.latimes.com/archives/la-xpm-1988-05-17-fi-2915-story.html. This link leads to an article on Cheryl Tatum.

Welsh, Kariamu. 1980. "Black Girls Can Shake Their Hair Now!" *Essence,* May 1980.

West, Cornel. *Race Matters.* Boston: Beacon Press, 1993.

Yarbrough, Camille. *Cornrows*. Carole Byard, ill. New York: Coward, McCann & Geoghegan, 1979.

Yarbrough's book was written for children, but all ages can appreciate it.

Government Documents and Journal Articles

Caldwell, Paulette M. 1991. "A Hair Piece: Perspectives on the Intersection of Race and Gender." *Duke Law Journal* 40, no. 2: 365-396. https://scholarship.law.duke.edu/dlj/vol40/iss2/5. (This journal article mentions Renee Rogers and Cheryl Tatum.)

California, Senate. Senate Bill No. 188 Discrimination: hairstyles. State Sen. Holly Mitchell. *California Legislative Counsel's Digest*. Ch. 58 (July 4, 2019). https://leginfo.legislature.ca.gov/faces/billTextClient.xhtml?bill_id=201920200SB188.

Dawson, Gail and Katherine Karl. 2018. "I am not my Hair, or am I? Examining Hair Choices of Black Female Executives." *Journal of Business Diversity* 18, no. 2: 46-56. https://doi.org/10.33423/jbd.v18i2.524. (This journal article mentions Renee Rogers.)

NYC Commission on Human Rights. *NYC Commission on Human Rights Legal Enforcement Guidance on Race Discrimination on the Basis of Hair*. New York City, February 2019. https://www1.nyc.gov/assets/cchr/downloads/pdf/Hair-Guidance.pdf.

United States Census Bureau, Historical Marital Status Tables. *Table MS-3. Interracial Married Couples: 1980 to 2002*. November 2018. https://www.census.gov/data/tables/time-series/demo/families/marital.html.

Interesting Web Sites

Braids by Breslin, http://www.braidsbybreslin.com

Breslin is a hair braider who constructs lace-front wigs, and teaches others how to construct them, too. I love why she does the lace-front wigs.

Center for Cultural Design, https://csdt.rpi.edu/culture/legacy/african/CORNROW_CURVES/culture/african.origins.2.htm
(also see the "/CORNROW_CURVES/culture/civil.rights.2.htm" link). This site has a wonderful history of braiding.

Christian Broadcasting Network, http://www.ob.org/orphanspromise/index.asp.

This page has been intentionally left blank.

Index

Symbols

Δ xiv, xv, 28, 31, 33, 34, 35, 36, 40, 44, 47, 61, 68, 70, 73, 75, 76, 78, 80, 83, 84, 85, 87, 88, 91, 125

A

Adams, Yolanda 25
African braiding xv, 43, 51
  As You Go extension method 51
  Under and Around extension method 47
  Under and Go extension method 49
Afro 25, 28, 34, 35, 44, 76, 78, 82, 130
Anatomy of a Hairstyle 96, 97
Ashford, Nickolas "Nick" 25
Autobiography of Malcolm X, The: As Told to Alex Haley 26, 132.
    See also Malcolm X

B

bad hair day 24. *See also* Kingsley, Philip
Black Girls Can Shake Their Hair Now! 25, 132.
    See also Essence; *See also* Welsh, Kariamu
braiding
  difference between African and French braiding 51
  hair braiding myths 29, 81
  hair in your comb 76
  hair loss 36, 40, 61, 71, 74, 84, 85, 126, 129, 132
  middle back area 40
  painful scalp 76
  reasons to braid hair 27, 69
  rebraiding 69, 70, 72, 73, 83, 128
  rubber bands 28, 69, 70, 71, 84, 104, 126
  same fiber 76
  terms 20, 21
  too tight 36, 40, 72, 75, 129
  types of hair used in 31
braids 21, 24, 25, 29, 30, 31, 40, 43, 44, 45, 53, 57, 67, 68, 69, 70, 72, 73, 74, 75, 76, 77, 80, 81, 82, 83, 84, 85, 86, 87, 95, 97, 98, 99, 104, 105, 107, 125, 126, 128
buildup 33, 68, 72, 73, 74

C

Chris Rock's documentary and Malcolm X 26
cornrows 20, 21, 126, 133
Cornwell, Dr. JoAnne 128. *See also* Sisterlocks®
Correctly Using Rubber Bands System 70, 126. *See also* CURB System

cosmetologist/cosmetology xiii, 86, 91, 92
  hairstylist 37, 61, 69, 80, 81, 83, 88, 91
  number one complaint concerning 81
CROWN Act, The 22, 26, 126
CURB System 70, 71, 84, 88, 126, 129
  seam ripper 28, 70, 71, 129
cut bulk 44, 53, 61

D
Dawson, Gail 22, 133
Derek, Bo 25

E
Ebony 24, 25
Essence 25
Ethiopian hairstyle 104

F
Feemster, Herb "Fame" 25
fiber 28, 31, 32, 44, 72, 74, 126. *See also* braiding
  bound end 32, 44, 125
  free end 32, 84, 125
  fresh fiber 28, 73, 75
  weight 44, 45, 70, 84, 88
first female millionaire. *See* Madam C. J. Walker
French braiding 51, 53
  As You Go extension method 57
  Under and Go extension method 55

G
Good Hair: Sit Back and Relax 25, 132. *See also* Rock, Chris
Green, Linda 25

H
hair
  broken 29
  combing 28, 33, 34, 35, 36, 37, 75, 76, 78, 83, 86
  experimenting with xii, xiii, 21, 27, 37, 43, 68, 72, 78, 86
  grease 28, 34, 70, 75, 84, 125, 128, 129
  greasing the scalp 77
  growth cycle 74, 87
  hair breakage xv, 36, 37, 71, 126, 127, 129
  hair types 126
  kinky hair 29, 127, 129
  line areas 36, 37, 126, 127
  nappy hair 128, 132
  oil 34, 70, 72, 77, 125
  resistance when combing 34, 35, 74, 75, 76

train, training 19, 29, 77, 84
wash (fiber and hair) 28, 32, 33, 34, 36, 37, 72, 73, 77, 83, 86, 87, 88, 127, 129
Your Hair Is Your Crown 23
Hair and Lines Test 37, 127. *See* also HALT
hair-esteem 24, 127
  bald-headed 24, 90
  I love my hair 27
  kinky hair 29, 127, 129
hairline 34, 75, 127, 129
hairstylist. *See* cosmetologist
Haley, Alex 26.
    See also Autobiography of Malcolm X, The: As Told to Alex Haley
HALT 37, 84, 88, 127
HOMEWORK
  about xvi
  exercises 43, 53, 92, 95

I

India 77
  oiling 77
italicized words xiv, 129
  base 47, 55, 67, 74, 126
  blunt cut 79
  bound end 32, 44, 125
  buildup 33, 68, 72, 73, 74, 125, 126
  Correctly Using Rubber Bands 70, 126
  CURB System 70, 71, 84, 88, 126, 129
  cut bulk 44, 53, 126
  extensions xii, 19, 20, 21, 29, 31, 32, 44, 45, 57, 61, 67, 68, 69, 70, 125
  fiber 28, 32, 44, 72, 74, 126
  free end 32, 84, 125
  Hair and Lines Test 37, 38, 127
  hairline 34, 75, 127, 129
  HALT 37, 38, 84, 88, 127
  kinky hair 29, 127, 129
  line areas 36, 37, 126, 127
  locs 68, 127
  main part 39, 88, 97, 128
  main sections 35, 36, 39, 97, 128
  matting 73, 75, 126, 128
  neckline 36, 37, 127
  perm xii, 80, 81, 84, 90, 126, 128, 129
  permed 27, 29, 33, 35, 36, 68, 78, 80, 83, 84, 128
  pressing xii, 34, 73, 128
  scrunchies 28, 70, 78, 129

seam ripper 28, 70, 71, 129
slice 40, 43, 44, 45, 47, 49, 51, 53, 55, 57, 74, 75, 84, 93, 95, 125, 126, 129
Smooth Up and Hold 36, 38, 129, 130
strands xv, 32, 43, 44, 47, 49, 51, 53, 55, 57, 59, 63, 65, 67, 68, 85, 93, 95, 127, 128, 129
strip 43, 45, 47, 49, 51, 53, 55, 57, 74, 93, 95, 129
SUAH 36, 37, 38, 84, 88, 129, 130
tight curls xii, 36, 126
tightly curled xii, 28, 78, 84, 129
too tight 40, 41, 72, 75, 108, 129
trim 35, 68, 75, 86, 87, 129
wash xi, 28, 32, 33, 34, 36, 37, 72, 73, 77, 82, 83, 86, 87, 88, 127, 129
water catchers 78, 129
wean 34, 129

J
Jet 24

K
Karl, Katherine 22, 133
Kingsley, Philip 24, 132

M
Madam C. J. Walker 132
main part 39, 88, 97
main sections 35, 39, 97
Malcolm X 26, 132
matted 68
matting 73, 75, 126, 128
Mitchell, Diana K. (experiences growing hair)
  a hacking motion to comb my hair 81
  cut out a perm xii
  dryness in my skin and hair 77
  from "some praying people" 23
  insisting on doing my hair myself 20
  it was an accident 44, 89
  my first exposure to braids 24
  my mother iii, ix, xi, 19, 20, 23, 24, 29, 77
  my relationship with God and Jesus Christ 90, 91
Mitchell, Holly 22, 126, 133

N
natural hair xii, 27, 32, 36, 80, 83, 132
  brushing 78, 88
neckline 36, 127
Newsom, Gavin 22, 126
New York City Commission on Human Rights 22, 26, 133

Nixon, Tricia 21
Norment, Lynn 25, 132
NOTE xiv, 32, 33, 35, 37, 44, 59, 61, 67, 68, 72, 73, 74, 75, 76, 80, 127, 129

P

perm xii, 80, 81, 84, 90, 126, 128, 129
plaiting
  extending plaits 61
  overhand plaiting 20, 57, 128
  overhand plaiting method 61
  Overplait plaiting extension method 65
  Preplait plaiting extension method 67
  underhand plaiting 20, 57, 128
  underhand plaiting method 59
  Underplait plaiting extension method 63
press/pressed/pressing xii, 25, 80, 128

Q

Quick Thought Check
  about xvi
  exercises xviii, 30, 38, 41, 82, 108, 130

R

Racism
  Hair and Discrimination in the Workplace 21
  I am not my Hair, or am I? Examining Hair Choices of
      Black Female Executives 22, 133.
      See also Dawson, Gail; *See also* Karl, Katherine
Richards, Janell Marie 25
Rock, Chris xv, 25, 132
  documentary 26, 27
Rogers, Renee 21, 22, 133
Rushen, Patrice 25

S

scrunchies 28, 70, 78, 129
  water catchers 78, 129
seam ripper. *See* CURB System
self-esteem 24, 127, 132. *See also* hair-esteem
  self-awareness xv
  self-confidence 24
Simpson, Valerie 25
Sisterlocks® 128. *See also* Cornwell, Dr. JoAnne
Slice, Strip, and Strands 94, 95
Smooth Up and Hold 36, 129. *See also* SUAH
SUAH 36, 37, 84, 88, 129
synthetic hair. *See* fiber

T

Tatum, Cheryl 21, 131, 132, 133
text-based learners/learning xv
  African braiding 43
  As You Go, African braiding extension method 51
  As You Go, French braiding extension method 57
  French braiding 53
   overhand plaiting 61
  Overplait plaiting extension method 65
  Preplait plaiting extension method 67
  Under and Around, African braiding extension method 47
  Under and Go, African braiding extension method 49
  Under and Go, French braiding extension method 55
   underhand plaiting 59
  Underplait plaiting extension method 63
Tolliver, Melba 21, 22, 131, 132
Tyson, Cicely 24, 25

U

United States Census Bureau
     "Table MS-3. Interracial Married Couples: 1980 to 2002" 20

V

visual-based learners/learning xv
  African braiding 42
  As You Go, African braiding extension method 50
  As You Go, French braiding extension method 56
  French braiding 52
   overhand plaiting 60
  Overplait plaiting extension method 64
  Preplait plaiting extension method 66
  Under and Around, African braiding extension method 46
  Under and Go, African braiding extension method 48
  Under and Go, French braiding extension method 54
   underhand plaiting 58
  Underplait plaiting extension method 62

W

water catchers. *See* scrunchies
Welsh, Kariamu 25, 132
Woodson, Julie 25
World Book Encyclopedia 20